Girls Know Best

Advice for Girls
from Girls
on Just about Everything

Written by Girls Just Like You!

Compiled by Michelle Roehm

Designed and illustrated by Marci Doane Roth

Gareth Stevens Publishing
MILWAUKEE

For a free color catalog describing Gareth Stevens' list of high-quality books and multimedia programs, call 1-800-542-2595 (USA) or 1-800-461-9120 (Canada). Gareth Stevens Publishing's Fax: (414) 225-0377.

Library of Congress Cataloging-in-Publication Data

Girls know best: advice for girls from girls on just about everything / written
    by girls just like you!; compiled by Michelle Roehm.
       p. cm. — (Girls know best)
    Originally published: Hillsboro, OR: Beyond Words Pub., © 1997.
    Includes bibliographical references and index.
    Summary: Thirty-eight different girls give advice on specific issues
including sisters, school, passing notes, adults, divorce, baby-sitting, boys,
sports, drugs, and personal appearance.
    ISBN 0-8368-2452-0 (lib. bdg.)
    1. Girls—Psychology—Juvenile literature. 2. Girls—Conduct of life—
Juvenile literature. 3. Girls—Health and hygiene—Juvenile literature.
4. Girls—Life skills guides—Juvenile literature. 5. Interpersonal
relations—Juvenile literature. 6. Children's writings, American.
[1. Girls—Psychology. 2. Conduct of life. 3. Girls—Health and hygiene.
4. Life skills. 5. Interpersonal relations. 6. Children's writings.]
I. Roehm, Michelle, 1968- . II. Series.
HQ777.G579   1999
305.23—dc21   99-13985

This North American edition first published in 1999 by
Gareth Stevens Publishing
1555 North RiverCenter Drive, Suite 201
Milwaukee, WI 53212 USA

This edition © 1999 by Gareth Stevens, Inc. Original edition published in 1997 by Beyond Words Publishing, Inc., 20827 NW Cornell Road, Suite 500, Hillsboro, OR 97124. Original edition © 1997 by Beyond Words Publishing, Inc. Additional end matter © 1999 by Gareth Stevens, Inc.

Book design and illustration: Marci Doane Roth
Gareth Stevens series editor: Dorothy L. Gibbs

The information contained in this book is intended to be educational and not for diagnosis, prescription, or treatment of mental and/or physical health disorders, whatsoever. This information should not replace competent medical and/or psychological care. The authors and publishers are in no way liable for any use or misuse of the information.

Printed in the United States of America

1 2 3 4 5 6 7 8 9 03 02 01 00 99

Foreword

Girls Know Best began early in 1996. To encourage girls to use their creativity and to take risks, Beyond Words Publishing, Inc. in Hillsboro, Oregon started a "Girl Writer Contest." Girls, ages 6 to 16, were asked to send in their best nonfiction ideas for a possible book.

The "Girl Writer Contest" ran in magazines and newspapers across the country, and the girls of America spoke up. Beyond Words received book ideas from girls by the bagsful. The hundreds of amazing stories and ideas received made it impossible to choose just one, so 26 favorites by 38 girl authors were compiled into *Girls Know Best: Advice for Girls from Girls on Just about Everything*.

A group of talented and passionate young women (all very recently girls themselves) collaborated with editor Michelle Roehm to make *Girls Know Best* the coolest book ever. Thanks go to Mary McMahon, Rachelle Stuckey, Margaret Langford, Amelie Welden, Anne French, and Marianne Monson-Burton, as well as to the parents, families, friends, and teachers who gave support and encouragement to the young authors. Thanks, also, to Dr. Mary Pipher for being an incredible catalyst and to Kerri Strug for getting involved with the project and inspiring girls around the world.

Special thanks go to all the girls who entered the contest. The writing received was truly inspiring, and each girl author has shown that achieving her dreams takes true dedication and a strong belief in herself.

If they can do it, so can you! Enter the "Girl Writer Contest" (see contest guidelines "Do You Want To Be an Author, Too?" and the "Potential Author Questionnaire" in the back of this book) or send your writing to other publications (see Katie Hedberg's chapter "Unlocking the Writer Inside You" for ideas).

Table of Contents

Introduction

Kerri Strug, age 19

✁ Hobbies: *working with children, charity work, sorority functions, arts and crafts, shopping* 📖 Favorite book: To Kill A Mockingbird ♬ Hero: *Mary Lou Retton* ❀ Dreams: *to become a good role model, mother and sports broadcaster. I have already achieved my dream of becoming an Olympic gold medalist.*

Kerri on ❀ Growing Up

I was born the third and last child in my family and will always be known as "the baby." When I was just a toddler, I always tried to follow my older sister, Lisa. I wanted to dress, eat, sleep and do gymnastics like her. I was afraid of the dark at night, so I would sneak into Lisa's room and beg her to let me sleep with her.

I used to dream about Nadia Comaneci and Mary Lou Retton. I begged my mom to buy me the movie *Nadia*, which I watched so often that I memorized all the lines and could turn off the sound of the TV. I dreamed of training with Bela Karolyi and being in the Olympics ever since I can remember. I always had the goal of becoming a great gymnast and role model, like Mary Lou Retton. I have made several different goals at different levels, in order to achieve that ultimate goal.

Overcoming ❀ Challenges

When I returned from the '92 Olympics in Barcelona, I was very upset about not making the all-around finals for the U.S. I decided to make a commitment to gymnastics for four more years so that I could achieve my personal goal to compete in the all-around and in the individual events. The fact that the 1996 Olympics were in Atlanta furthered my desire to continue gymnastics.

While training for national and world competitions in '93, I suffered a career-threatening muscle tear in my stomach. I was beside myself when the doctor told me it would take 6-8 months to heal. I started physical therapy immediately. Gradually, over the six-month period, I began to improve and finally returned to gymnastics.

This recovery took more mental energy and commitment than I ever realized I had inside of me. But the feeling of accomplishment made it all worthwhile.

Believing in Yourself and Achieving Your Dreams

When most of us are little girls, we dream about being movie stars, athletes and mothers. When we reach our teenage years, we suddenly realize that we don't have the same dreams and we often feel lost. This is the critical time to set new "specific" goals, make a list or plan for how to achieve them and start working toward these goals. In addition, we must always persevere and work hard without giving up or becoming discouraged. Our attitude must change from the little girl dreaming about the future to the young woman working in a positive, energy-filled effort to achieve her goals.

My best advice for you is: Believe in yourself. As I stated in my new book *Landing On My Feet: A Diary of Dreams*, the most important factor to achieving your dreams is your attitude about yourself.

First, ask yourself do you really want to achieve your dream or are you trying to satisfy your parents or coaches? Second, how hard are you willing to work for your dream—what sacrifices are you willing to make? School life, friends, playtime and other things may need to be cut back to give more time to your dream. Third, do you feel in your own mind that you have the talent to achieve your dreams—do you believe in yourself? Having the desire and talent isn't enough to succeed. You have to believe in yourself.

It took me many years of hard work and continued commitment with a positive attitude to finally convince myself that I really "believed in myself" and I was not just listening to someone else's dream. Once I attained this level of self-belief and confidence, I benefited from my efforts beyond my wildest dreams. Your attitude about yourself is the key to personal success and is much more important than pleasing others or winning an event.

Have fun with this book. These authors are proof that if you take steps toward your dream, you can achieve it. You can see that you are part of a powerful, talented group of young women around the country and around the world. If we believe in ourselves, we can do anything!

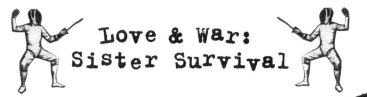

Love & War: Sister Survival

Rebecca Rushing, age 13

✀ Hobbies: *sketching, piano, postcard collecting, cooking, reading, softball* 📖 Favorite books: *the Redwall series* ☹ Pet peeve: *when someone interrupts me or isn't listening when I have something important to say* ❀ Dream: *to open a successful restaurant in a big city*

Melissa Rushing, age 7

✀ Hobbies: *soccer, softball, football, basketball, baseball and tennis* 📖 Favorite author: *R. L. Stine* ☹ Pet peeve: *when someone steals my candy* ♙ Heroes: *Shannon Lucid, my mommy, and my sister Rebecca* ❀ Dream: *to be an astronaut*

You can never get rid of your sister, no matter how hard you try. And believe us, we've tried! We're sisters and we know all about being rivals and best friends, all at the same time. We wrote this chapter to pass on a little smidgen of our experiences to those of you who may be having sibling troubles.

Getting Some Privacy

Privacy is always an issue between sisters. Being a girl is hard work, and sometimes you just need to be by yourself. So, how to shake off your sister? Here are a few suggestions:

◆ If you have your own room, try to get it into your family's heads that when your bedroom door is closed, it means knock before entering or, if possible, not entering at all. If just talking to them won't work, try putting a sign on your door.

◆ Go to the library and check out your favorite book. You can read it there—a lot of libraries have lounge areas, and it is a quiet place where you can get peace.

- Tell your sister that you'll be doing something she hates, and if you hate it, too, do something else. This might not work for a very long time, but we suggest giving it a try.
- Go on a bike ride.
- Get involved in activities after school, like joining a sports team or taking lessons in something you are especially interested in.
- Simply ignore her. She may not like it, but it works. Sooner or later she'll leave you alone. Just don't go too far, such as talking about her while she's still there.

Getting Time with the 'Rents

Sometimes you need to spend time with your 'rents without your sis. When we spend time alone with our parents, we can get some good talking done or maybe just enjoy their company. Different families might allow for this in different ways. We know some who set aside regular time slots and some who do it in little ways, like cooking dinner or going fishing.

Melissa: I like to spend time alone with my parents because Rebecca isn't there to steal their attention from me. I go to the movies with both of them and I go shopping with my dad in bookstores while Rebecca goes to the mall with my mom.

Rebecca: To get away with my parents, I go shopping with my mom or spend a few hours with my dad at his bookstore or eat lunch with one or both of them. Melissa hates shopping, so I am ensured that these times will be and stay mine.

Snooping

What if you suspect your sister of going through your private things? Try to give her the benefit of the doubt. For those of you who don't know, giving someone the "benefit of the doubt" is when you say someone is innocent until they are proven guilty. Like when a judge lets someone who has been accused of a crime go because nobody has evidence that they were the one who actually committed the crime. So if you accuse your sister of stealing your diary, but you think that *maybe* you left it at your friend's house, let her go. Check first, sentence later.

Fighting

She drives you crazy! You fell for one of her stupid tricks again! You just want to kick her! Every sister we know has at least a couple of times when they have wanted to yell and scream and tear each other's hair out. Older girls often wish to wring their sister's neck for reading their diary or invading their privacy in some other way. Younger girls normally feel horribly left out when their older sisters don't let them play with the "bigger girls." These feelings are totally normal.

Rebecca: Sometimes she gets really annoying. My biggest pet peeve is when she procrastinates or gives up on something or doesn't do something she's promised. She then leaves me to do whatever it was.
Melissa: I hate it when Rebecca gets mad at me, bosses me around or doesn't play with me. When we fight, she won't listen and she's really mean.

Fighting is a painful experience, but if you can do it so that you don't hurt each other too much, emotionally or physically, you will be better off. Sometimes talking about your problems, not yelling, with someone who doesn't live in the house helps you calm down. Or, heaven forbid, try to see her side.

Rebecca: I've found that writing down what is bothering me helps me to get it out of my system easily. I just keep a spiral notebook by my bed, and when I get really mad at her, I write all of my feelings and then tear it up and throw it away.
Melissa: When Becca and I fight, we yell at each other. Sometimes I hit her and she hits me. Then we talk to my dad, because we need a problem solved. He says, "Leave your sister alone. One of you go upstairs." It takes

us about two hours to make up and then we shake hands (never hug) and go play.

Sharing

Letting a sibling, one who has torn up something of yours before, use your things can be a hard decision. And you should know from experience that she normally won't treat it with the same care you would.

Melissa: We don't share our things very well. I don't like Becca using my stuff; I'm afraid she'll mess things up or lose pieces.

So what's a girl to do? Learn not to be stingy with your less-treasured stuff and protect your special stuff. And understand that you have to let your sister borrow some of your things if you ever expect to borrow things from her. A suggestion: when she borrows something of yours, write down what it was and have her sign it. Then give the piece of paper to your parents or put it in a safe place. That way, you have proof that she did in fact get it from you, and she can't say that it was hers to start with. Lots of girls have trouble sharing with their sisters, and they eventually figure out how to make this problem disappear.

Rebecca: We have a sort of understanding. I don't take things of Missy's without permission, if she does the same.

Melissa: I think that to share better we could talk together about how we want the other person to use whatever they want to use.

Dealing with Her Friends

If you are anything like us, we're sure you have friends over to your house regularly. The problem is, sometimes sisters have a little trouble dealing with each other's pals.

Melissa: Her friends always try to trick me into thinking they're not lying. They treat me like a baby; they act like I'm stupid. I'm not! I'm smarter than them!

What to do? Well, try staying away from your sister and her friends if they are mean to you. Maybe, if your sister is bugging you or showing off while your friends are there, try to get your parent(s) to get her off your backs.

Melissa: She's good at leaving my friends and me alone; she doesn't bug us.
Rebecca: When my friends come over, sometimes she's OK and leaves us alone. The rest of the time she shows off and we have to make her leave. If she would stay away, like I always do when her friends are over, maybe she wouldn't get her feelings hurt.

Fun Times Together

Perhaps you have your best times together when you have just made up from a fight. Or maybe shopping. Any time, any place, when all is peaceful with your sister, you are feeling good. So how to keep it that way? We're not sure. But to keep the good times rolling, we do know one word that sums it all up: COMPROMISE!!!

Melissa: I had a great time cooking dinner with my big sister. It was fun because she let me do most of the things. I got to use my new cooking tools and she showed me how to do different things.
Rebecca: Sometimes my sister can be the greatest. Like when we've just made up from a fight. She is really nice and we have a lot of fun. We bake cookies or play outside or do a special project.

Doing stuff with your sister is sure to bring you closer. What you choose to do together really depends on what you like. If you play basketball and have a hoop in your yard, maybe you could play "horse" or have a one-on-one game. Or maybe you could play some other sport together, like tennis or "catch." Perhaps you could walk to a nearby park, go to the movies or play a board game. The Internet has some neat sites that include craft ideas, games to download or puzzles.

Here are just a few that we found:

- Kid's Cooking Club, at www.kidscook.com
  This site has cool and easy recipes that you can print out.
- Electric Origami, at www.ibm.com/stretch/EOS
  This site includes kaleidoscopes, puzzles and other brain teasers.
- Aunt Annie's Craft Page, at www.auntannie.com
  This one has lots of wonderful craft ideas and very good ideas for rainy days.
- Dr. Seuss, at www.afn.org/~afn15301/drseuss.html
  This site has terrific graphics and fun games to download.

You and your sister could also try some of the crafts and activities included in the chapter in this book titled "What to Do on Those Boring Days."

GrowOlder

Beth and Sandra are grown-up sisters and live far away from each other now. They still get together once in a while and do something away from everyone else, but they miss each other and wish they would've enjoyed their time together more when they were younger. They took that time for granted.

Beth: We need to get away together because we both have kids and husbands and jobs, and those things distract us from staying caught up on each others' lives. Once, we met halfway between our homes, stayed in a hotel and Christmas shopped. We probably spent more time talking and laughing and telling stories than anything else. It was great!

Everyone gets older. When you grow up, it's hard to keep up with your sister. Before you know it, she's married or expecting a baby, and you may ask yourself where the years went. Believe it or not, you'll miss each other. That's why it's important to do things together now and to do things that you'll be able to look back on and laugh about. Sisterhood is a very special relationship, one that needs preserving.

Home-made Beauty Recipes

Sarah Van Raden, age 14

✀ Hobbies: *rafting, snowboarding, playing drums* ☹ Pet peeve: *when people constantly go on about people they don't like*
♬ Heroes: *my mom and Sheilynn Wactor, from the musical* Stomp!
❀ Dream: *to touch the lives of young people while I teach kindergarten and play the drums*

Katie Van Raden, age 12

✀ Hobbies: *soccer, reading, chess, climbing trees, having fun!*
✎ Favorite class: *Math* ☹ Pet peeve: *when someone talks behind your back, instead of saying what they feel* ♬ Hero: *my mom*
❀ Dream: *to be a vet*

We have both experimented with beauty products, but found they were expensive and too harsh on our skin. Our chapter started one day when Sarah got a zit. Desperate for a cure, she asked Mom for help. Mom dug up her old HIPPIE beauty book from the '60s—it was under the love beads and polyester bell bottoms! We found lots of quick, natural remedies for pimples and realized how simple it would be to make our own. For a couple of years we've been creating recipes and experimenting on friends, family and ourselves. The result is this collection of recipes we think you'll enjoy. It's a fun way to spend time with friends, sisters and even Mom.

For Blemishes

Zap Your Zits

After washing your face at night, make a paste of 1 Tbsp. white sugar and a couple of drops of water. To Use: Dab onto blemishes and leave on overnight. (Folk medicine followers believe that sugar has an anti-bacterial quality).

• The paste we made out of sugar not only took the redness out of the blemish, but by the end of the day it was hardly noticeable.

The Baking Soda Blues for Blemishes

Mix 2 Tbsp. baking soda with enough warm water to form a soft paste. To Use: Massage onto blemished skin and leave on for 15 min. Rinse with cool water.

• A good treatment for all skin types.

Facial Cleansers

Sweetie Wheatie

Mix whole milk with enough wheat germ to form a soft paste. Add a small amount of honey and mix well. To Use: Rinse face with warm water, then gently massage mixture onto damp face. Rinse with warm water, then rinse with cool water.

• Gentle face wash for normal to dry skin.

You're Nuts!

Mix 2 Tbsp. finely ground almonds, 2 Tbsp. oat flour and 1 Tbsp. chamomile tea (dry). To Use: Place 1 Tbsp. of dry mixture in hand and mix with olive oil or warm water to form a paste. Massage gently over moist skin. DO NOT SCRUB. Rinse with warm water, then cool water.

• Gentle face wash for normal to dry skin.

Milk Maid

Put 1 Tbsp. rosemary in a cup of cold milk. Let it sit for 2 hours. Strain and refrigerate. To Use: Rinse face with warm water. Shake the milk cleanser, dip a cotton ball in and wipe face. You may need to use more than 1 cotton ball. Rinse with warm water, then cool water.

• Skin freshener for all skin types.

√ Doin' the Cornmeal Scrub

Mix 1-1/2 Tbsp. yellow cornmeal and 2 Tbsp. plain yogurt in the palm of your hand. To Use: Gently massage onto face. Rinse with warm water, then cool water.

• Face cleanser for oily skin.

√ Time to Face Your Oatmeal

Mix 2 Tbsp. finely ground oatmeal, 2 Tbsp. wheat bran and 2 Tbsp. honey. Mix in enough olive oil or apple cider vinegar to form a soft paste. To Use: Rinse face with warm water. Apply cleanser and gently massage. Rinse with warm water, then cool water.

• When mixed with olive oil, this is suitable for normal to dry skin. When mixed with vinegar, this is suitable for normal to oily skin.

Facial  Masks

√ Sticky Situation

Warm 1 Tbsp. honey. To Use: Gently massage onto clean face. Lie down with feet slightly elevated for 15 min. Rinse with warm water, then cool water.

• Suitable mask for all skin types.

Wear a Good Breakfast

Mix 1 Tbsp. plain, natural yogurt and 1 Tbsp. honey. Place 1 jasmine, peppermint or chamomile tea bag in 1/2 cup (120 ml) boiling water. Let this steep 20 min. Remove tea bag and add honey-yogurt mixture. Stir well. Add 1/4 cup (35 g) finely ground oatmeal. To Use: Apply to face and gently massage. Leave it on for 15 min. while you lie down with your feet slightly elevated. Rinse with warm water, then cool water.

Sweet Appeal

Steam a peeled, cored apple. Mash and mix with 1 Tbsp. honey and 1 Tbsp. whole milk. To Use: Apply to clean skin and leave on for 15 min.

It is best to lie down with feet slightly elevated during this time. Rinse with warm water, then cool water.

• Suitable for all skin types.

Banana Fana Fo Fana

Mash 1/2 ripe banana. Add 1 Tbsp. honey. To Use: Gently massage onto face. Lie down with feet slightly elevated for 15 min. Rinse with warm water, then cool water.

Hair  Care

The Hairy Rosemary Fairy

Place 1 Tbsp. rosemary into 1 cup (240 ml) hot water. Let steep 20 min. Strain and cool. Add 2 Tbsp. avocado oil, 1 Tbsp. castor oil and 2 eggs. Whisk together till frothy. To Use: Massage conditioner into hair and scalp. Wrap hair in towel for 20 min. Shampoo and rinse in normal way. Make fresh for each application.

Monster Mash

Chop 1 medium size avocado in the blender until smooth. Add 1 Tbsp. olive oil. Blend well. To Use: Massage into hair and scalp. Wrap hair in plastic wrap and leave on for 10 min. Rinse with warm water. Shampoo and condition as usual.

Hold the Mayo

Mix 1/2 cup (120 ml) regular mayonnaise with 1 Tbsp. fresh lemon juice. To Use: Massage into hair and scalp. Cover hair in plastic wrap for 10 min. Rinse with warm water. Shampoo and condition as normal.

Sage Brush

Simmer 1 Tbsp. sage and 1 black-tea bag in 1/4 cup (60 ml) apple cider vinegar and 2 cups (480 ml) of water for 30 min. Strain and cool. To Use: Shampoo as usual and then rinse with solution. Will add shine to dark colored hair.

Sun Kissed

Mix 1/4 cup (60 ml) fresh squeezed lemon juice with 1/4 cup (60 ml) cool water. To Use: Rinse hair with solution and sit out in the sun until your hair is dry. Be careful not to get this in your eyes. Tip your head back while pouring juice onto hair. Let the extra run off away from face. Shampoo and condition as usual. Will add blonde highlights to light colored hair.

Bath Products

Wilbur's Buttermilk Bath

Mix 1 cup (240 ml) buttermilk, 3 Tbsp. Epsom salts and 1 Tbsp. canola oil. To Use: Pour entire solution into running bath water. Soak as long as you can get away with it.

Down by the Seashore

Mix 3/4 cup (150 g) Epsom salts, 1/4 cup (50 g) sea salt, 1/4 cup (35 g) baking soda and 1 Tbsp. vanilla or rum extract. To Use: Pour entire solution into running bath water and pretend you're on vacation.

Pine Tree Pamper

Cover 1/2 cup (35 g) fresh pine needles with 1 cup (240 ml) boiling water. Let this steep for 20 min. To Use: Pour into large bowl. Add enough warm water to cover your feet. Soak your feet and enjoy!

Just For Fun!

Chocolate Lip Gloss

In a microwave-safe dish, combine 3 Tbsp. cocoa butter, 4-5 chocolate chips and the oil from one small capsule of vitamin E. Microwave for 30 seconds. Stir. Microwave another 30 seconds and stir again. Continue microwaving at 30-second intervals, if necessary, to melt the chocolate chips. Blend ingredients with a spoon until smooth. Put in a small container and refrigerate until solid. Use on lips. (You'll want to eat it 'cause it smells so good, but we don't recommend it!)

School Daze

Katie Test, age 12

✂ Hobbies: *reading, French horn, OM, keychain collecting, pottery* ✎ Favorite class: *Drama* ☹ Pet peeve: *people correcting me—I hate it!!* ♫ Hero: *Sojourner Truth*
❀ Dreams: *to be a guidance counselor and to live in NYC*

Anne Lancaster, age 12

✂ Hobbies: *reading, talking on the phone, making things with paint and clay, decorating my room* 📖 Favorite book: The Immortal *series* ☹ Pet peeve: *when people get what they want by whining* ♫ Hero: *Superwoman*
❀ Dreams: *to write a fiction book and go to Africa*

We know you're nervous—who isn't? Come on, you're starting school again and you're freaking out! When we recently started middle school, we were totally clueless. We needed help—majorly! That's why we decided to write this chapter: to give you advice on how to handle homework, grouchy teachers and even stubborn lockers. Here's all you need to know about school after a long summer. Read on, girl!

Your  First Day

Your first day is VERY nerve-racking. If you're like us, you'll want to know everything about everything. Here's how to handle it.

The Night Before

Put a good head on your shoulders—meditate, read, write in your journal, do whatever it takes to get yourself calm. Pack your lunch (make it big) or get out your lunch money. Make sure you have your lock for your locker, your notebooks, pencils, pens and whatever else you think you might need or is on the school supply list your teacher may have sent you.

Have your outfit picked out the night before or you will take forever in the morning trying to figure out what looks good on you. (This sounds like something your mom would say, but it helps.) Then SLEEP!

The Morning of Your First Day

Wake up 45 minutes to an hour before you need to leave, in order to be well prepared. Get dressed, eat a huge breakfast and stay calm. Write your bus number and your locker combination on the back of your hand. Be at your bus stop (if you ride the bus) 15 minutes earlier than the scheduled time.

Once at School

Arriving at school can be a very big deal, so step off the bus or out of the car as if you go here every day of your life. Walk into school and go to your assigned area or wherever administrators tell you to. When you get there, portray lots of confidence. If you're walking into a room of complete strangers, smile, throw back your shoulders and act as if you do this every day. (Don't throw your shoulders back too far—you don't want to look like a snob.)

Find a seat somewhere in the middle of the room next to a girl who looks like she doesn't know anyone, or if you can't find one of those, then just sit with a girl. Be friendly, but not too pushy. If you see someone you think might be a cool person to be friends with (guys, too) or that you know, go over and say hi or smile across the room when you catch their eye. Remember, they're nervous too—waving or smiling can give them a friendly face to look for. If you don't see either or if whoever you are sitting next to doesn't want to talk, pull out a book, a comic book, a magazine or something to keep you busy until class starts. Once class has started pay close attention—your teacher will have lots of things to say, pass out and go over.

Now if you thought that was hard, wait till lunch! Just kidding—it's not as bad as you think. You've probably talked to and made acquaintance with someone by now—they're your best bet on who to sit with. If you haven't met anyone yet, find someone who looks alone or nice and set your tray down there. If the seat is saved, say "Okay" and move along, walking tall and with confidence. Lunch will soon become your favorite period.

After School

The rest of the day should go pretty smoothly. By the end of the day you should be WORN OUT!!!!! Get in the bus or car and go over what you need to do before you sleep. Make sure you watch for your stop! Once home, make yourself a small snack (Look in the "Freaky Foods" chapter for this one!). Get everything signed, do your chores and SLEEP!!! Remember, this day we've described is a worst-case scenario. Usually it's not that bad.

Classes

Each of your classes should range from 30 minutes to 2 hours, depending on your school. Sometimes even 30 minutes can seem like hours. When a class is boring or unclear, you might wonder whether you're really learning anything. Sometimes you don't feel comfortable asking questions. In a case like this, ask your question privately—before or after class is a good time. If you need help, ASK FOR IT! You don't need to be embarrassed—everyone needs help sometimes. If you can't get the help you need or if you feel you're not getting it when you ask for it, you've got to do something. Talk to your parents and maybe they will talk to the teacher or principal. If this doesn't help, try writing a sincere letter to your principal.

One question everyone asks about classes is "How hard is the work?" That depends on your working habits. If you wait till the last week to do a month-long project, then yes, it's hard. If you do your project on schedule, then no, it usually isn't. Our best advice is to stay on top of things.

Getting  Around

Getting from class to class is a *big* issue. On the first day, or even the first couple of weeks, it can be difficult to remember which is next, science or social studies. We completely recommend writing your schedule on the back of your hand. If you don't want to ruin your natural beauty, then write it on an index card to carry around with you. In a dull moment, run through or quiz yourself on your schedule.

Sometimes it's hard to make it to classes on time, especially when you have to coordinate trips to your locker in between. How do you do it? With brains! We suggest devising a locker schedule. Figure out which classes you can get to on time, while going to your locker in between.

Sometimes getting your locker open can slow you down, too. The only advice for that is practice, practice, practice. Practice your locker combination and actually opening your locker ahead of time. The more you practice, the faster and easier it will be. If your lock sticks (as ours did a million times), try spinning the combination as slowly as you can. This may drive you insane if you're in a hurry, but, trust us, it works.

But even with a locker schedule and practice opening your locker, you'll probably be late to class sometimes, and being tardy usually has its consequences. There are some good excuses for being tardy (like having your book bag spill out all over the stairs), but you might need someone to vouch for you if you use them.

Teachers

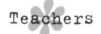

Obviously, teachers can be a major cause of stress in your life. But they most likely have good reasons for the decisions they make. You might think it was unfair of Mr. Barker not to give you an extension, but he may think it's not fair to give you one when you've had the same assignment and the same amount of time as everyone else to complete it.

All teachers have rules, such as no talking, no chewing gum, no sharpening your pencils in class, etc. It's only going to hurt *you* if you break their rules. Now, I know you're not going to be silent during class, but you don't have to throw spitballs whenever your teacher turns around. Don't test their limits—it doesn't take much to get on their bad side.

The most important thing to remember is that teachers are people too, and they do have personalities and lives beyond their teaching. Your teachers are usually cool people, so don't take them for granted. If they are good teachers, respect them.

Homework/Managing Your Time

You know that pile of books you carry around in that thing called a book bag? Good. They've got a reason. No, not to make you miserable or to make you suffer (though they do!). They're to give you practice on what you learned in class.

You know how it is when what you learned in math class is perfectly understandable until you get home and hit the books—you start the even numbers on page 407 and it seems like Greek? What do you do? You can go buy a notebook especially for math notes. Then tomorrow take notes explaining what you covered in class. If it still seems like Greek, see if you can set up a tutoring session before or after school. Don't be afraid to go— it can't hurt! You can also ask any stupid or embarrassing questions you couldn't ask during class. Other good sources for homework help are your friends, parents or boyfriend. They may know more than you think!

But what if you get what's goin' on, but you've got voice lessons, play practice and swim team tonight? How do you cram it all in there? Try squeezing in your math on the way to swim practice, after play rehearsal. Then do your social studies before your voice teacher comes in. If using every spare moment of time for your homework doesn't help, you're proba-bly going to have to drop something. Is gazing at Jerry and Jack the only reason you tried out for the play? Is gabbing with Julie all you're on the swim team for? Decide what activities are least important to you and drop one soon, before your grades start plummeting.

Got the ZZZZZZZZZ's when you're doing homework? Here are some helpful hints to keep you from dozing off:

+ Reward yourself—every time you finish a chunk of work, eat or watch TV.

+ Take breaks—do little things like practice guitar or feed Spot.

+ Size up the scene—make a list of the homework for the night, then cross it off every time you finish something. You can see the list being devoured.

+ Read out loud—pretend you're teaching it to someone else or giving a speech. This may help you understand it better and catch mistakes.

- Listen to music—some people concentrate better that way.
- Time yourself—make it a competition to see how quickly you can do a problem. Set speed goals for yourself, like a runner.

Now hit the books, girl!

Gossip

"Hey, did you hear that John goes with Kim and that Zach likes Maggie?" This is one of the basic conversations you might hear while you're charging down the hall at top speed. Gossip is a main topic in school. You're not being especially bad, naughty or evil if you gossip, but when you obsess over it, you get really annoying.

Gossip also may not be as good as you thought it was. When you tell someone something you heard, you usually don't think about the person it's about, until it's about you. When you tell your best friend a secret, they tell their friend and the chain goes on and on. When you find out, you feel awful! Gossiping can also get you into trouble—big trouble. If you blab something you're not supposed to blab, you can lose a friend's trust and even the entire friendship.

Some kids are totally into gossip, while others prefer to stay out of it. It's really your choice.

Conclusion

School is fun—really. At school you see "that guy," your best friends and your favorite teachers. Think how BORING life would be without it! The best overall advice we can give is to act friendly and be cool, confident and calm. Go out there and reach for the stars . . . the worst that can happen is your belly button shows!

How to Pass Notes in Class
Without Getting Caught!

Shayne Blauner, age 16

✄ Hobbies: *sports, postcards, swimming, shopping, talking on the phone* ⊗ Pet peeve: *I hate being dirty — even a speck makes me nervous.* ♪ Hero: *my mom* ❀ Dreams: *to become successful in all matters and enjoy life*

Esther Levy, age 16

✄ Hobbies: *swimming, drawing, dancing, taking pictures*
✎ Favorite classes: *Phys. Ed., Communication*
❀ Dream: *to forever have peace, health, and happiness*

Esther: *One afternoon Shayne passed by me nonchalantly in class and dropped a small folded piece of paper on my desk.*

Shayne: *I wondered if Esther had gotten my drift to read the note, when I saw her foot next to me with a small piece of paper sticking out of her shoe. I took it.*

Esther: *Next I heard a long sigh as Shayne stretched her arms up behind her and dropped a crumpled note onto my desk.*

Shayne: *We realized that we had spent over 20 minutes passing notes in class and never got caught! So we created more and more exciting ways to pass notes. We are pretty experienced now and still almost never get caught.*

The Football Pass

(if your friend sits in front of or behind you)

1. Write your message.

2. Fold it in a rectangular shape.

3. Place it half-way sticking out of the side of your shoe.

4. Move your foot in front or behind you and lightly kick your friend's foot to let her know about the foot message.

Pen Pal Pass

1. Write your message.

2. Fold your paper so it's really small and narrow.

3. Place it in the cover of the pen.

4. Casually say to your friend, "Here's the pen you wanted." Give her a
wink so she gets the hint.

Chain Gang Pass

1. Write your message.

2. Crumple a piece of paper into a small ball.

3. Write "Please pass to _____ ." on it.

4. Cautiously hand the ball of paper to the person who sits next to
you. If she isn't a "goody-goody" she'll pass it along.

Stretch Pass

1. Write your message.

2. Crumple the note into a ball.

3. Place the ball inside your hand and make a fist.

4. Sit up straight, stretch your arms upward and make a yawning
sound so the stretch seems real.

5. Once your hand is up over your friend's desk, drop the note.

Tissue Issue Pass

(if your friend has a tissue box)

1. Casually ask your friend for a tissue.

2. Take out a tissue and write your "issue" on it.

3. Fold the tissue back to its original form.

4. Take out another piece of tissue and actually blow your nose, just
to make the act seem real.

5. Put the note-tissue back in the box and say, "Thanks, here's your
box back." (Give her a wink.)

Cannonball Pass

1. Write your message.

2. Be sure your teacher is writing on the board.

3. With extreme caution, throw the note to your friend.

Goody-Goody Pass

1. Ask your friend if you can see her notebook to catch up on the notes.

2. Write your message on the margin of a piece of paper inside.

3. Say, "Thanks, here's your notebook back." (Give her a wink.)

Soccer Field Pass

1. Write your message.

2. Crumple it up into a ball.

3. Place it on the floor and kick it over to your friend when your teacher isn't looking.

Fly Away Pass

1. Write your message.

2. Fold it into the shape of a plane.

3. When your teacher isn't looking, quickly fly the plane across the room to your friend.

Notebook Billboard

1. Write your message on the front/back of your notebook.

2. Raise the notebook to your eye level as if you're reading.

3. Leave it this way for a minute or so, while your friend reads the message, then bring it back down.

How to Avoid Life's Most Embarrassing Moments

Zoya Ahmadi, age 14

✂ Hobbies: *guitar, listening to music, exercising, going out with friends*   📖 Favorite author: *Mark Twain*   ☺ Pet peeve: *rejection (guys, grades, etc.)*   ♬ Hero: *Courtney Love*   ❀ Dream: *to be a U.S. Supreme Court Judge*

I wrote this chapter because I know being embarrassed in public is one of the worst things girls have to face. Most of the stories and advice are common sense, but most girls forget all about common sense when they're caught in a humiliating situation. Hopefully, you will realize that these tragedies happen to everyone and you'll learn to laugh at yourself. Each of these stories is true, but the names of the people have been changed to protect them from further humiliation.

If you want to avoid life's most embarrassing moments, DON'T EVER...

... fall asleep in class if you have a habit of snoring.

Rebecca was a good student, but one time she had stayed up all night studying for a test. She fell asleep in class, and when the bell rang, she woke up to find she had been snoring and the whole class was staring at her.

... make eye contact with someone you like and then look at your friends and start laughing.

Urcella had a crush on Martin for months and constantly stared at him, hoping to make eye contact. Finally, when they did, she looked at her friends and accidentally laughed. Martin thought she was so immature that he never looked at her again.

. . . walk into a bathroom without looking at the sign first.

Jeremy was going to hang out with Samantha at lunch. On his way to meet her he rushed into a bathroom, assuming it was the guys'. He quickly saw he was in the wrong bathroom, but as he walked out he bumped into Samantha. She thought he was a pervert, so she never talked to him again.

. . . be rude to a stranger who cuts you in line.

Shirly was standing in line at school when a guy cut in front of her. Shirly yelled at him, only to realize her crush, Nathan, was right behind the guy. It turns out the guy she yelled at was Nathan's best friend.

. . . turn and walk quickly without looking where you're going.

Janet was arguing with Lydia in front of a major group of people. Janet wanted to leave the argument with a dramatic exit, but when she turned around and started walking away, she tripped over a crack in the sidewalk and almost fell.

. . . pretend to like the same things your crush likes just to impress him.

Sandy liked a guy named Justin, whom she barely knew. But she did know Justin's best friend, so she would casually ask him what kind of music Justin liked, what sports, etc. She found out he loved rap, so next time she talked to Justin and he asked her what kind of music she liked, Sandy lied and said rap. She started babbling about the artists she liked, who were R&B artists, not rap artists. Justin automatically knew she was faking and told her he didn't like talking to fakes.

. . . laugh so hard that you snort!

Tracy and Monica were in the hallways joking around when Tracy cracked a really funny joke. Monica laughed so hard that she snorted really loud. As she snorted Jonathan walked by and started imitating her.

. . . forget to check that you're all buttoned or zippered up.

Gabrielle finally got up the nerve to ask Eric to go to a movie with her. She got up her courage, walked up to him and started talking. Everything was going well until she noticed that he wasn't paying attention to what she was saying. When she asked what was wrong, he explained that two of her blouse buttons were undone and her bra was showing.

. . . write something really embarrassing in a note.

Tracy and Connie were the biggest gossips at their school. During class, they passed a note between them about how the government should fire teachers who don't know how to dress (specifically, their teacher). In mid-pass, the teacher grabbed the note from Tracy's hand and read it aloud! He was so angry that he made them wear their PE clothes for the rest of the day because "their shorts were too short." Connie and Tracy never criticized anyone about their clothes again!

. . . speak in a foreign language unless you know exactly what you're saying.

Debra studied Chinese for a year to prepare for a summer exchange program. Unfortunately, she forgot to study the correct dialects spoken in the different parts of the country. When she got off the plane, she tried to make conversation with her driver. Instead of asking him what places in the area he would recommend she visit, she told him he looked like a sausage and should get a nose job! The driver turned around and told her in English what a rude young lady she was!

Freaky Foods

Rivky Thaler, age 14

✂ Hobbies: *reading, exercising, talking*

✎ Favorite class: *Phys. Ed.* 📖 Favorite writers:
Robert Frost, Lucy M. Montgomery ☻ Pet peeve:
big shots and haughty people Ⅎ Hero: *my mother*

❀ Dream: *for everyone in the world to live in peace and harmony*

Deena Abend, age 14

✂ Hobby: *reading* ✎ Favorite classes: *Art and Phys. Ed.* 📖 Favorite
writer: *Louisa May Alcott* ☻ Pet peeve: *people who think they are g-d's gift
to mankind* Ⅎ Hero: *my mother*

We picked this topic because, as you know, you are what you eat. We think that if you eat interesting foods, cause and effect, you'll be an interesting person. So go ahead, interest others and interest yourself. Enjoy!

Faulty  Fruits

What You Need

FOOD

any 12 pieces of fruit your
    mom doesn't need, preferably:
    cherries, peaches, plums or strawberries
whipped cream
water enough to cover fruits
1/2 cup (100 g) of sugar

UTENSILS

pot
spoon
blender

What You Do

1. Put all your fruits with the water into the pot on low heat.

2. Let cook for about 45 min. to 1 hour.

3. When it's finished cooking, add sugar.

4. Cool till it's at room temperature.

5. Put in blender till no bumps remain.

6. Serve in pretty bowls, topped with whipped cream.

Serves 15 kids.

Peanut Butter Pieces

What You Need

FOOD	UTENSILS
1 chicken breast, cleaned and cut into	baking pan
bite-sized pieces	bowl
3 Tbsp. spicy Chinese peanut sauce	spoon
3 Tbsp. peanut butter	
2 Tbsp. soy sauce	

What You Do

1. Mix peanut butter, soy sauce and spicy Chinese peanut sauce in bowl. Taste mixture and add ingredients to your taste.

2. Put the chicken in the pan.

3. Pour the sauce over the chicken and cover completely.

4. Cook for 45 min., covered, at 350 degrees Fahrenheit (175 degrees Celsius).

5. After 45 min. uncover chicken and cook for another 30 min.

6. Serve on nice plates.

Serves 4 kids.

Savory Strawberry 'n' Spinach

What You Need

FOOD	UTENSILS
1 10-oz. (280-g) package of spinach	1 large mixing bowl
1 carton of strawberries	1 container with a lid
2 Tbsp. sesame seeds	mixing spoons
5 Tbsp. honey	
3 Tbsp. vinegar	

What You Do

1. Wash strawberries.

2. Slice strawberries and put in bowl with spinach.

3. Pour honey, vinegar and sesame seeds in the container with a lid and shake well.

4. Pour dressing over strawberries and spinach, then serve.

Serves 7 kids.

Vicious  Veggies

What You Need

FOOD	UTENSILS
3 carrots, sliced	frying pan
1 can baby corns	spoon
1/2 cup (70 g) chopped scallions	baking sheets
5 Tbsp. soy sauce	
1 tsp. lemon juice	
12 puff pastry shells	

What You Do

1. Grease frying pan.

2. Place carrots, scallions and baby corns in frying pan on medium heat.

3. When vegetables are nearly cooked, add soy sauce and lemon juice.

4. Put on low heat and stir until completely cooked.

5. Place pastry shells on the baking sheet and follow the directions on the package.

6. When pastries are done, let cool and fill with vegetable mix.

7. Heat again before serving.

Serves 12 kids.

Zesty  Zucchini

What You Need

FOOD

2 cups (400 g) brown sugar

3 large eggs

1 cup (240 ml) vegetable oil

1 tsp. vanilla extract

1 tsp. baking soda

1 tsp. salt

1 tsp. cinnamon

1 tsp. allspice

3/4 tsp. ground cloves

1/4 tsp. baking powder

2 cups (280 g) grated zucchini

3 cups (420 g) flour

3/4 cup (150 g) chopped walnuts

UTENSILS

electric mixer

greased 8x12 inch

(20x30 cm) pan

What You Do

1. Preheat oven to 350 degrees Fahrenheit (175 degrees Celsius).

2. In mixer combine sugar, eggs, oil, vanilla, baking soda, salt, allspice, cinnamon, cloves and baking powder.

3. Add the zucchini, flour and walnuts. Mix again.

4. Pour the batter into the pan and bake for about 1 hour or until a toothpick comes out clean.

5. Remove cake from the oven, let cool and cut into squares.

Serves 8 kids.

Girls in Sports

Megan Myers, age 11

✦ Hobbies: *guitar, soccer, basketball* 📖 Favorite writer: *Edgar Allen Poe* ☺ Pet peeve: *when people tease me about being short* ♪ Heroes: *Rosie O'Donnell and Lisa Leslie* ❀ Dreams: *to meet Rosie O'Donnell and have her as a friend; to become a good DJ, know my music and be nice to my listeners*

Alexandra Moffet-Bateau, age 11

✦ Hobbies: *skiing, horseback riding, reading, basketball, collecting seashells, getting letters* ✎ Favorite class: *History* 📖 Favorite writer: *Virginia Hamilton* ☺ Pet peeve: *hair in the sink* ♪ Heroes: *my mom and Sheryl Swoopes* ❀ Dream: *to become a horse vet or a journalist or a politician*

We play on a basketball team together. We want girls to know that it's okay to be a girl and to play sports. We want to get the message out that girls are not the weaker sex—we are equal. Sports are important to us because they not only show what we girls can do, but what we can achieve. They teach us to have commitment and use teamwork in whatever we do. Sports build self-confidence and self-esteem. For example, at the start of the season many girls on our basketball team were afraid to even dribble the ball down the court—now they're starters! But the main reason we like sports is because they're FUN!!!

Health  Benefits

When a person is physically active, she is more likely to have a healthy, positive image of herself. Sports help your mind and your body to be stronger, which increases your self-esteem. Did you know that girls who do sports in high school are more likely to get better grades and go to college than girls who don't?

When our mothers were little girls, they were highly discouraged from doing sports by their parents and schools. Girls who excelled in sports were called names like "tom-boy" or told that they were "unlady-like." Alexandra's mom avoided gym as much as possible and never learned how to swim. Because my mother never participated in sports or learned to enjoy them, it is hard for her to find an activity that will help her keep in shape and stay healthy. Now everyone realizes that it is absolutely important to exercise if you want to remain healthy.

Even if you are physically disabled or have health challenges, you can still play sports and be physically active. Ask your doctor or go to your local Y for some suggestions on what you are physically and mentally ready to do. If you have asthma, don't be afraid to play sports and don't use it as an excuse not to. Look at Jackie Joyner-Kersee—she has asthma and she's a world famous track star. Consult a doctor, pace yourself according to your ability and don't forget to have any medication you may need with you at all times. Exercise will most likely improve whatever health problems you have.

Another benefit of doing sports is that it can keep you from becoming depressed. The most pessimistic people in the world are the ones who sit around and do nothing all day. Girls who play sports are less likely to suffer from depression. Joining a sports team or exercising on your own should help your mental as well as your physical health. If you join a sports team you'll have more to do than just sit around and watch TV. You'll have a healthier and more active social life. So go out there and find the sport that best fits you!

Individual Sports vs. Team Sports

Individual sports and team sports each have advantages and disadvantages. Some advantages of individual sports are:

- If you win, you get all the credit and the glory.
- You don't have to deal with ball hogs.
- You don't have to feel bad if you're not the star of the team.
- You don't have to worry about your team members being late for a

game or not being prepared.

- If you play badly, you're not letting your whole team down.

Some disadvantages are:

- The whole game depends upon you instead of a whole team. If you lose, it can be a lot worse.

- You miss the fun of bonding with your teammates, sharing the glory of the wins and the agony of defeats.

Some advantages of team sports are:

- It's not just one talent, but many talents that make up the team. You learn how to cooperate with other people.

- The game is not your responsibility alone.

Some disadvantages are:

- If you are the star of the game, your teammates may envy you.

- If someone else is the star, you may feel jealous of her.

Are You a Team Player or a Solo Star?

Here's a quick quiz to help you determine if you'd be happier in a team or individual sport. **Write your answers on a separate piece of paper.**

1. Do you need a lot of rest periods?

    A) Yes   B) No

2. You were the star of the game. When someone asks how the game went, you say:

    A) "The game went really well. My team did great."

    B) "It was my best game ever."

3. It's half-time and your team's losing. You:

    A) Give them a pep talk to rally the team together.

    B) Spend time practicing alone so you'll play better the second half of the game.

4. During a basketball game you're dribbling toward the basket. Your shot is blocked, but your teammate is open. You know she's not as good a shot as you. You:

A) Pass her the ball anyway and cheer her on to make the shot.

B) Keep the ball and try to make the shot yourself.

If you have more "A's" than "B's" you'd probably be a better fit for team sports. If you have more "B's" than "A's" you might try an individual sport instead.

Good & Bad Sportsmanship

A good sport . . .

. . . congratulates the opposing team when they win.

A bad sport . . .

. . . cries, has a temper tantrum or refuses to congratulate the opposing team when they win.

Bad sportsmanship doesn't do anything for your image or what people think of you. It makes people feel bad, and sooner or later you'll find yourself without any friends. On the other hand, good sportsmanship makes people feel good, makes them want to play with you and gives you a good image. You'll also find yourself with many friends.

Dealing With a Bad Sport

Having to deal with bad sportsmanship is a big pain, and we hope you never have to deal with it. Unfortunately, almost everybody does. If you ever find yourself with a bad sport, block them out of your mind and ignore them. Otherwise you'll just be giving them the attention that they crave.

Usually people are bad sports because they have low self-esteem, they feel pressure from an adult or they think that having an attitude is the only way to be respected. If you think one of these may be the reason for bad sportsmanship with someone you know, it may help to talk it over with them. When you do confront them, try to bring out their positive side first.

Are You a Bad Sport?

If you're a bad sport, don't be afraid to admit it and don't feel too bad, because it is a curable disease. The first step is admitting it to yourself. Then you can start working on it. Ask one of your best friends to remind you when you start to act un-sportsmanlike. When they do remind you, don't get mad at them. Otherwise, you'll just find yourself sitting on the bench watching your team play.

We know that nobody likes to lose but it is very, very, *very* important to be a good loser *and* a good winner. Recently our team was a finalist in a basketball tournament. Though we thought we were being treated unfairly by the referees and we did not win the game, we were good sports and congratulated the winners. Later, some of us got together and talked about the game, which was a much better way of dealing with our frustration than yelling at the refs. Talking over the loss made us more determined to improve our game so that we could beat this team the next time.

Before the game you should always say to yourself that even if you're down by a score of 50-4 (which we have experienced), you will not be a jerk to the other team, the refs, your coach or anyone else. When you're upset, it's easy to get out of control and hurt someone mentally or physically. If you look at most sports injuries that occur, they are caused by someone being out of control.

Making Mistakes

If you're human (which we hope you are), you're going to make mistakes. But it won't kill you. Do you ever feel like if you make a mistake your parents, your coach or even your teammates will get mad at you? Well, sometimes that does happen. Instead of them yelling at you, ask them if you could talk about the good things that happened and not so much about the bad things. But don't completely ignore the bad things. Talk about them, too, and see what you could do better next time.

Is it unfeminine to play sports?

NO WAY!!! Playing sports is a different way of expressing ourselves, different from any other way! Sure, you can take dance and express yourself gracefully and sure, you can play an instrument and express yourself musically, but when you play sports you are showing the world what you can really do.

Some of you are saying, "But if my boyfriend sees me all sweaty and yucky he won't go out with me anymore." Now first of all, if you have a boyfriend who's only interested in the way you look and not your personality, then you need to dump him. And second of all, if he really likes you, he'll respect what you do and cheer you on!

Are there any sports girls shouldn't play?

We don't know of any. If a girl wants to wrestle, let her wrestle; if a girl wants to play hardball, then let her play hardball. There is no sport that a boy can play that a girl can't play, too.

Are boys better at sports?

In general, no. Maybe it just so happens that a boy is the best all around sports player in a school. That doesn't mean there isn't a girl somewhere who is better than him; it just means he is the best at his school. And maybe somewhere at another school it just so happens that a girl is the best all around sports player. That doesn't mean some boy somewhere isn't a better player than her; it just means she's the best at her school. So you see, we're all equal!

Do you think boys and girls should play on the same team?

Alexandra: I think it would be OK if girls and boys played on the same team, until maybe age 11, when girls start to develop and the boys start to get muscles. Then it gets a little bit awkward.

Megan: I think that if they want to play together they can, but when they get to the age where girls feel at a disadvantage, they should have the choice to change or not. I, for instance, played on a boy's hardball team for three years until I was 11, then switched to an all-girl's team.

Why do guys get to play pro and girls don't?

Megan: I think it's because people think that girls aren't as strong as boys athletically.

Alexandra: I think it's because a lot of sports are male dominated. But it doesn't have to be that way. Now we have a women's basketball league, the W.N.B.A. So if you ever want to go pro, follow your dreams, work hard and GO FOR IT!!

Is it fair that male athletes earn more than female athletes?

Alexandra: No, I don't think it's right at all. Female athletes probably work twice as hard as the men. They're trying to build a place in the sports world for us, the future generation of athletes.

Megan: What they should do is lower the men's salaries and raise the women's so they would make the same.

Conclusion

We hope we have helped you think about sports in a positive way. If you have been a bad sport in the past, perhaps our suggestions will help you to overcome that. And don't forget, no matter what happened in the past, girls can rule sports, too!

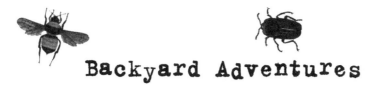

Backyard Adventures

Hazella Bowmani, age 13

✄ Hobbies: *drawing, reading, playing computer games, writing*

📖 Favorite books: The Giver, The Fifth of March *and* The Child of the Morning ❁ Dream: *to become a producer, cartoonist, author, artist or president of a big company*

Years ago, in Girl Scouts, I went on a camping trip, which turned out to be exciting and interesting to me. Recently, I wanted to experience that feeling again, so I decided to camp in my backyard. Not only was the idea closer to home, but it saved my parents from driving me somewhere far away. Follow these instructions and experience wonderful and exciting adventures in your own backyard.

Camping Out

What you need

- a tent or old sheets, a long string/rope and 2 big garbage bags
- a sleeping bag (pad or air mattress for underneath is optional)
- enough bottled water to drink and some for cooking
- food that's not heavy (chips, pizza slices, hot dogs, etc.)
- plates and eating utensils
- old margarine containers with lids
- a journal or notepad and pen or pencil
- stuff for bird watching (see "For the Birds")
- stuff for insect watching (see "For the Bugs")
- stuff for nature activities (see "Flower Pressing" and "Leaf Rubbings")

Setting up camp

Set up your tent or make one (see below) and unpack the things you'll need, like food, your journal or book. Spend some time really getting to know your surroundings and writing your thoughts and feelings.

How to make your own tent

Find two trees that are at least 5-6 feet (1.5-1.8 m) apart. Tie your string from one tree to another, about 3-4 feet (1-1.2 m) up the tree trunks. Lay your sheet across the string, so it hangs evenly down both sides with both edges touching the ground. Use sticks or rocks for tent stakes, to keep the sheet edges apart like a triangle. Lay down your garbage bags inside and put your sleeping bag on top of them to keep your bed dry.

Making 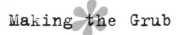 the Grub

If you are going to cook something, pour some water in the containers, put the lids on and leave them in the sun. If you are heating something up, wrap it in foil and put it in the sun for a LONG time (5 hours).

For the  Birds

For those of you who think bird watching sucks, did you know that people pay hundreds of dollars to see birds migrate, establish territory and all the other neat things birds do?

What you need

1. notebook or your journal
2. pen or pencil
3. optional—bird guide book & binoculars

While you're outside, keep an eye out for birds. If you have binoculars, use them. When you see a bird, make a drawing of it—don't forget its colors and any interesting markings. If you have a bird book, look it up and write what kind of bird it was.

For the  Bugs

Have you ever sat in a stuffy classroom and had to watch a ladybug inside a glass jug, and the teacher says to observe how it acts in its natural environment? Well, guess what? That's not its natural environment and it's not going to act *natural*.

What you need

1. notebook or your journal

2. pen or pencil

3. optional—magnifying glass & insect guide book

Find a good place where there are a lot of insects, get out your paper and for about a half hour stay in one place and draw, record, label and try to identify each insect you see. Try to figure out where its head, eyes, antennae, abdomen, legs, etc. are and label them on your drawing.

Flower  Pressing

What you need

1. flowers

2. wax paper

3. an iron (Get a parent's help for this part.)

Gather flowers and put them between two sheets of wax paper. With help from a parent, take a hot iron and move it lightly around on top of the wax paper for about 5 seconds. This will seal the flowers inside. You can also press flowers in your journal for a few days to dry.

Leaf  Rubbings

What you need

1. paper

2. crayons

3. leaves or other flat, textured objects

Leaf rubbing is fun, and you don't only have to use leaves. You can use anything flat, like a coin, tree bark, flowers, etc. Put the object under the paper and rub over it really hard with a crayon. Voilá—a beautiful work of art!

How to Deal with
Mean, Grouchy, or Just
Plain Ornery Adults

Jaclyn "J.J." Jenkins, age 14

✄ Hobbies: *reading, playing clarinet, talking, taking pictures, singing, traveling* 📖 Favorite writer: *Louisa May Alcott* ☹ Pet peeve: *when people are inconsiderate of others' feelings* ⌧ Hero: *Aunt Patty* ❀ Dream: *to become a good lawyer in either family or criminal law*

Carrie "C.C." Smith, age 14

✄ Hobbies: *reading, writing, listening to music, singing, dancing* ✎ Favorite classes: *Math, Science, Social Studies* ☹ Pet peeves: *people who lie and people who ignore me* ⌧ Heroes: *Rosie O'Donnell, Rachel Carson and my teacher, Rhonda Peterson* ❀ Dreams: *to become an architect or a lawyer and to write*

In our chapter we hope to give you a lot of information and a few laughs, too. We're pretty sure (in fact almost positive) that, at some time, you will use the advice given in this chapter. We sure have.

What Drives You Crazy About Adults?

Adults do a lot of things every day that grind on our nerves. Here are some of the things that really make Mrs. Ruth's second period Humanities class steam up. Thanks, guys!

When they . . .

Play favorites   Are power hungry   Are unfair   Yell

Are negative   Treat you like kids   Are unreasonable

Give too much work   Bad-mouth kids

Are overprotective   Think they know it all   Don't listen

Avoid talking to kids   Bring up things continuously

Change their minds   Punish

Par ents

Yes, we know that parents aren't the only kind of adults, but we also know that kids seem to get in the most trouble with them, so we figured this would be a starting place. To understand parents, we need to figure out how they think. We did this by making up general parent types.

The parent types are (drum roll, please): pushy parents, unconcerned parents, politically correct parents, distant or over-worked parents and median parents.

Pushy parents are the lovely parents who want you to give 110 percent of yourself. They're the kind that don't realize that good is sometimes as good as it gets. This character type can be good because they make you push yourself, but oftentimes they push too hard.

Unconcerned parents tend to go in the other direction. They pretty much let you run wild, which can be fun, but when you need some pushing, they are of little assistance.

Politically correct parents are the masters of the community. They may have some horrible problems, but to everyone outside the family they're "just fine." Politically correct parents aren't bad people, they just tend to care more about what other people think than their children's feelings, worries, morals or preferences.

Overworked or distant parents may seem like bad parents, but in fact, they may not really be. They miss a lot of what is going on in their child's life because they are trying to give their kids a better life.

Median parents are a mixture of all the other groups, but not so much that it's a bad thing. They're also called median parents because it's what many parents are, including ours.

Teachers

Did you realize that most of us spend 1/4 of our day, five days a week, four weeks a month, nine months a year with teachers? Hmmm? Well, we do. And since we spend all this time with them, it's just common sense to have a chapter about them.

"Give them the teacher types, Carrie."

"Another list? Do I have to?"

"All right, all right . . . I'll do it myself."

"The teacher types are: grouchy teachers, prejudiced teachers, near-retirement teachers, untested teachers, too-nice teachers and true teachers."

Grouchy teachers are often the kindest teachers you'll ever have, but they have a gruff exterior. To really enjoy your classes with them, you have to look behind that gruff area.

Prejudiced teachers. We don't mean racially prejudiced, we mean teachers who base their feelings for people on their popularity, their intelligence, their participation in sports, their parents' income or job, their choice of clothing or anything else besides how much that person wants to learn.

Near-retirement teachers are teachers who figure they've served their time and are just waiting for the Social Security checks to come. In their hearts, they care about the students, but they don't teach you much because they're just biding time.

Untested teachers pretty much will let you do what you want. They, like near-retirement teachers, probably do want you to learn, but they have no idea what they are doing and let kids get away with way too much.

Too-nice teachers are so sweet they make you sick. Often they don't punish kids because they don't want to be thought of as "mean." Unfortunately, they are being "mean" to those kids who want to learn.

True teachers are what we think of as an endangered species. These teachers want you to learn and are truly happy when you do. Grouchy teachers often fit into this category.

Other  Adults

Now we come to the big one! Adults as a whole. Kinda scary.

"You know what I hate, Carrie? You know when you go to the store and you ask for help and they ignore you? It makes me sooo mad! And then, while you're looking around, they always watch you, like you're going to steal something. Do they do this to adults? Nooo."

"I hate it when people on the telephone ask to talk to my mom or dad, especially when I call them. I feel like saying. 'No, but you can talk to me. Remember me, I'm the one who called you!'"

"Have you noticed that 99.9% of the time waiters will look to adults first when asking for orders?"

"Or how about when you're in your own yard and the mailman comes up and won't give you the mail until he gets an adult to verify that you live there—like you'd lie about a thing like that!"

"My Uncle Mike pulls my hair and teases me because he knows it bugs me. He pretty much will do anything if he knows it will bug me."

"Jackie, do you know what I hate about relatives?"

"What, Carrie?"

"They never let any embarrassing story die. They just keep on telling it for life. It's so embarrassing and annoying."

"Why don't you just tell them it bothers you?"

"Are you kidding? They would just ignore me."

"Maybe it's not the stories that are the problem, maybe it's your reaction."

"Excuse me?"

"Did you ever stop to think that maybe they tell those stories *because* they bother you so much?"

"Well then, what should I do?"

"You've heard the saying 'I'm not laughing *at* you, I'm laughing *with* you?' Try laughing at yourself! Try to see the humor of the story!"

"And if I can't?"

"Act if you have to. There are also two other options."

"And what would those be, Dr. Jackie?"

"You could quickly answer questions and then switch the conversation over to an embarrassing topic about the person who ratted on you."

"Ah . . . sweet revenge."

"Or . . . beat 'em to the punch. Tell the story before they get to it. That way it won't be half as embarrassing."

What to Do When Adults Tick You Off

"We have to remember, Jackie, that parents sometimes get mad at us for a reason."

"Whose side are you on?"

"Jackie, you can't honestly believe that you're totally innocent of annoyance. The main thing to remember is to keep your cool with adults."

"I know what you mean, Carrie. In fact, one strategy I like to use is the 'Put-Myself-In-Their-Shoes Plan'. For instance, when my aunt's yelling at me, I think of how I would feel if we were to switch places. Often my reactions would be much more drastic than hers. What's your strategy, Jackie?"

"I go for the 'I-Plead-The-Fifth' strategy, because most of the time when we argue I try to remain quiet until I'm as far away as possible."

"Carrie, while that's a good 'now' strategy it's really not solving the problem, and holding in anger is *never* a good thing."

"Jackie, you asked me for my strategy and I gave it to you, but I guess you might as well spill the rest of your anger management plans."

"Thank you, I was getting to that. One way is called 'Open-Up-Your-Feeling-And-Your-Pores.' When some people get mad, they get physical. Running, playing a sport, biking or even walking are all healthy ways of getting rid of your anger, Carrie."

"Another strategy is 'Clean-Up-Your-Anger.' Do something constructive; cleaning, cooking, gardening or rearranging are all good things that you can do that will help someone, and *you*, in the process of releasing your anger, Jackie."

"Our last strategy is called 'Go-Back-In-Time.' To do this, you play back the situation so that both of you know exactly what happened. This strategy is good for sorting out small skirmishes, but isn't good for major battles. In that case, you'd want to let your parents cool down for a little while."

Bridging the Gap: Getting to Know Grown-Ups

Earlier we said many of the problems between adults and kids are caused by lack of communication. Bad communication can really mess up your family ties, which are about the most important things this life has to offer. Plus, we will be dealing with adults all our lives. Learning to get along is very important. A big part of good communication is getting to know each other. Here's a way to test how well you know your parents (or other important adults in your life).

The Parent Comunication Test

This test should help you see how your relationship with your parents rates. **Write your answers on a separate piece of paper, then check with your mom or dad to see how many you have right.** Good luck!

1. What's your Mom/Dad's favorite movie? *(2 points)*

2. What's your Mom/Dad's favorite animal? *(2 points)*

3. What's your Mom/Dad's favorite food? *(2 points)*

4. What's your Mom/Dad's biggest pet peeve? *(3 points)*

5. How old is your Mom/Dad? *(1 point)*

Here's the scale:

(**9-10**)   Wow! Your communication lines are up and in full operation. You're doing great.

(**8**)   Sometimes your lines get crossed, but you can pretty much hear each other.

(**7**)   Get your connections checked because you're coming in faintly!

(**6 or less**)   Your communication lines are down. Make an effort to get to know your parents better. Do things with them now and then. Ask them questions. If you make an effort, chances are they will, too. Try to fix those damaged lines. It's still not too late.

BIG Words You Can Use to Impress Friends, Parents and Teachers

Katie Arnold, age 13

✂ Hobbies: *magic, reading, acting, writing, dancing*
✍ Favorite class: *Math* 📖 Favorite book: Dealing with Dragons 😣 Pet peeve: *when people put the ingredients of a taco in the wrong order* ♜ Hero: *Eleanor Roosevelt*
❀ Dream: *to become a professional musical theater performer or a magician*

Kyra Borg, age 13

✂ Hobbies: *reading, writing, soccer* ✍ Favorite class: *History*
📖 Favorite books: Lord of the Rings *and* Sophie's World 😣 Pet peeve: *when the dog messes up the trash, and I have to clean it up*
♜ Hero: *Emily Dickinson* ❀ Dream: *to become an archaeologist*

We chose this topic because we both love language and wanted to share with you many people's favorite, bizarre and unheard-of words. Though many times while writing our chapter, we felt like defenestrating it, it is finally done. Sprucing up your vocabulary can be fun when talking to your friends or useful when writing a report. Whatever your purpose, we hope you enjoy our chapter and find it ameliorates all your problems.

Ambergris (ám ber gri): *a grayish, waxy substance from the intestine of a sperm whale*

"Ugh, this lasagna looks like it's covered in *ambergris*!"

Ameliorate (a méel ee o rate): *to improve*

"Mrs. Charlie, you could *ameliorate* my stress level by eliminating homework."

Bumptious (búmp shus): *crude, loud, assertive, pushy*

"I can't stand your boyfriend. He's so *bumptious*!"

Compunction (cum púnk shun): *a feeling of guilt or regret*

"I feel such *compunction* for eating my sister's M&Ms. Or maybe it's just a stomachache."

Conundrum (ko nún drum): *a puzzling question or problem*

"I can't figure out whether this toothpaste cap screws on to the left or the right. What a *conundrum*!"

Corpulent (córp you lent): *fat, large*

"I just inhaled that chocolate mousse . . . I feel so *corpulent*."

Coruscate (córe us kate): *to glitter*

"Bobby's so perfect, when he smiles, his teeth just *coruscate*."

Defenestrate (de fén uh strate): *to toss through a window*

"You are driving me crazy. Would you just go *defenestrate* yourself please?"

Deracinate (de rás in ate): *to pull up by the roots*

"The principal was so mad at me she *deracinated* her hair."

Duress (doo réss): *compulsion by threat or force*

"I only ate the turkey Tetrazzini under great *duress*."

Elucidate (ee loóse ih date): *to explain or make clear*

"You're so stupid. Shall I *elucidate* the problem for you?"

Exonerate (ex ón er ate): *to clear—as of an accusation, etc.*

"I'd be happy to *exonerate* you, Sis, for a small fee of $10."

Fastidious (fas tíd ee us): *critical, hard to please*

"Mrs. Acorn is so *fastidious*, I had to rewrite my paper five times!"

Faux pas (fóe pa): *a social blunder*

"What a *faux pas*! I told someone I actually *like* Geometry."

Frivolous (fríh vo lus): *lack of seriousness or sense*

"Mom, you are acting so *frivolous*. Please come down off the couch, okay?"

Gargantuan (gar gán chew in): *gigantic, huge*

"What a *gargantuan* favor you are asking. I just don't think I can staple that for you. I mean, what's in it for me?"

Jink (jink): *to move swiftly or with sudden turns*

"Now don't forget, team—never blink when you *jink*."

Kibitz (kíb its): *to give unwanted advice, especially while others are working or seriously discussing something*

"Quit your *kibitzing* and come help me already."

Kismet (kíz met): *fate, destiny*

"Is it my *kismet* to be forced to eat this spinach soufflé?"

Lambaste (lam bást): *to scold severely*

"I should *lambaste* you for stealing my multi-colored pen."

Lassitude (láss ih tude): *weariness of body or mind from strain*

"But Mrs. Magura, I was in such a state of *lassitude* I couldn't possibly find the strength to finish the homework assignment."

Loquacious (low quáy shus): *talking a lot, fond of talking*

"Kyra is so *loquacious* I can never get her off the phone."

Magnum opus (mág num ó pus): *a person's great work, their masterpiece*

"Mr. Stone, this is my best paper ever. It is my *magnum opus*!"

Masticate (más ti kate): *to chew*

"Can you believe it? All through lunch Peter was *masticating* with his mouth open. Gross!"

Mercurial (mer cúre ee al): *changeable, fickle*

"Oh Jenny, you're so *mercurial* when it comes to yogurt."

Noxious (nók shus): *harmful to living things*

"Cafeteria food is so *noxious*, especially this 'Mystery Meat.'"

Nutate (néw tate): *to nod one's head*

"I'm totally answering your question. I am *nutating*."

Pernicious (per nísh us): *causing destruction or injury*

"My little brother is so *pernicious*. You should see what he did to my cat."

Perspicacious (per spi káy shus): *having a keen mind*

"Oh Dad, you're so *perspicacious*. I hope to grow up just like you. Now, how about that allowance raise?"

Pretentious (pre tén shus): *claiming excellence or importance*

"Katie is so *pretentious*, just because her mother won that Nobel Peace Prize. I don't see what the big deal is anyway."

Purloin (per lóin): *take dishonestly, steal, pilfer*

"Perhaps I should *purloin* my report card and burn it before my mom sees my grades."

Pusillanimous (pew sill án ih mus): *showing a lack of courage*

"Ryan is so *pusillanimous*, he fainted during the math test."

Quaff (kwaff): *drink deeply*

"May I please *quaff* your V-8?"

Quandary (kwán dree): *in a dilemma, worried, perplexed*

"I am in such a *quandary*. I can't decide whether to use the red marker or the green one."

Quidnunc (kwíd nunk): *a gossipy person*

"I heard from Bill, who heard from Susie, who heard from Jane, that Margo is a total *quidnunc*."

Roister (róy stir): *revel noisily*

"When our friends get together, we always *roister*!"

Serendipity (sair en díp i dy): *good luck, good fortune*

"Mrs. G, it is so *serendipitous* that I bumped into you today. Now about that grade. . ."

Soporific (sop or ríf ik): *causing sleep*

"What a *soporific* class! I could barely keep my eyes open."

Sycophant (síke o fant): *a suck-up, one who flatters others to gain something*

"My sister is such a *sycophant*. Wait till you see her Mother's Day gift."

Transmogrify (trans móg ri fy): *to change shape*

"My dog, Pepito the Chihuahua, *transmogrified* into an evil beast when I hid his favorite toy."

Viscous (vís kus): *sticky, thick*

"This is some *viscous* macaroni. Did you put glue in it?"

Xerostomia (zi row stów mi a): *dryness of the mouth*

"Dad lectured me for so long, it's a wonder he didn't get *xerostomia*."

Yeuk (yook): *to itch*

"You *yeuk* my back, I *yeuk* yours."

Zoanthropy (zo án thra py): *a mental disorder in which one believes oneself to be an animal*

"Emma was so crazy in class today. I swear she must have *zoanthropy*."

Survival Guide for Divorce

Marie Hansen, age 14

✂ Hobbies: *singing, community service, pageants*
☹ Pet peeve: *people who don't care about themselves or their future* ☐ Hero: *Hillary Clinton* ✿ Dreams: *to go to Yale and study music and politics. Then to sing professionally and be a model. Then to become the first woman president of the U.S.*

Ellen Hansen, age 12

✂ Hobbies: *acting, modeling, writing, swimming*
✎ Favorite class: *Language Arts* ☐ Hero: *Eva Peron*
✿ Dream: *to be a successful doctor*

Laura Hansen, age 10

✂ Hobbies: *violin, dance, reading, collecting dolls*
📖 Favorite writer: *Roald Dahl* ☹ Pet peeves: *my sisters and hand-me-downs* ☐ Hero: *my mom* ✿ Dream: *to be a violinist and a dancer*

"My parents decided to say 'I don't.'"— Laura

If your parents are going through a divorce, you will see many changes. Some of them will make you laugh, some of them will make you cry and most of them will make you scared and a little queasy in your stomach. We've heard adults say that change is hard for most people. We think it's hardest for kids. After all, we've barely had time to get used to things the way they are now! Besides, our parents are the part of our lives we depend on. How do you depend on something that is changing, especially if you don't know what it's changing into?

Our parents got divorced nine years ago, so we've grown up watching them fight, divorce, remarry and learn to get along. We've learned a lot about grown-ups and divorce, and we think we can help you.

What is divorce?

Marie: It's when a married couple decide they would be better off without each other. It's hard for everyone involved.

Ellen: But often it can be a change for the better in the long run.

Why do people get divorced?

Laura: Because they don't like each other as much as they did before.

Ellen: They are changing or they have changed.

Marie: Each situation is unique and has its own set of reasons. Most reasons are too complicated and adult-related for parents to share with their children. That's good. There are some things we really don't need to know! Don't be afraid to say that to a parent who is telling you things about the other parent that you think are none of your business (but say it nicely!).

My parents are always fighting. Does this mean they are going to get a divorce?

Laura: Maybe. If they are not getting along, it may be best for everyone— even you.

Ellen: Maybe or maybe not. You can't really tell by watching them. They spend time alone together and you don't know what that is like. It's scary when parents fight, but it's usually not as bad as it seems.

Marie: Fighting is a very natural thing. You fight with your siblings and your friends when they get on your nerves. If you think your parents are fighting so much they might get a divorce, ask them. Tell them what you observe. They might not be able to give you a complete answer, because they may not be sure, but at least they'll know what you're observing and how you're feeling.

IMPORTANT NOTE: If your dad is hitting your mom, that is wrong. No matter how much you love your dad, you have to realize that he shouldn't hit her and you should support your mom in leaving him and going somewhere safer. Although it may be the hardest thing you'll ever do, you should tell your teacher, principal or school counselor that your dad is hitting your mom.

I'm scared about my parents' divorce. What can I do?

Laura: It's okay to be scared. I was scared when my parents got divorced. Just hang in there!

Ellen: Your parents aren't spending as much time with you and they might be cranky. That doesn't mean they don't love you. They need some space and some time.

Marie: Of course you're scared—it's a scary thing. Think about why you are scared. Let your parents know what you are thinking. They can reassure you. They're scared too, but you can all support each other.

Can I make my parents get back together?

Laura: No, and don't try. If they stay together, they won't be happy and they'll probably just fight.

Ellen: No. Lots of kids probably try, but it won't work, so don't get involved doing something that will just frustrate everyone.

Marie: Just like us, our parents have to choose their own paths. You can't do anything that will get them back together. It's their problem and their jobs to make life work for themselves. The decision to divorce is probably not something they made in a hurry. They've likely thought about all of the possibilities and they see this as the best thing to do.

Is it my fault that my parents are getting divorced?

Laura: No. How could it be? They're the grown-ups, you're just a kid.

Ellen: No. This is between your parents. There's nothing a kid could do that would cause a divorce.

Marie: Of course not. You might think so, because the families on television seem perfect and that's what you want. But families aren't perfect. Neither are you, but you can't make parents stop loving each other or get a divorce.

Do my parents still love me?

Laura: Yes. They may not spend as much time with you while the divorce is going on, but they will always love you.

Ellen: Your parents will always love you. It's just that during the divorce they are sad, angry, tired and scared. Sometimes it's hard to act lovingly when you feel all of those things.

Why do my parents have to go to court?

Ellen: Divorce is a legal situation, just like marriage. So if your parents want to end their marriage, they have to do it in court. With some divorces, only one parent goes. In others, both go. It usually takes just one day in court, but if there are many things your parents are disagreeing about, they may have to spend many days there. The judge is helping them figure out how to divide assets (things they own like a house, cars, furniture, savings, etc.) and how to work out custody.

Marie: In a divorce, your parents go to court to decide who gets what, including custody. If they are fighting about custody, you might have to go to court. If you do, the attorneys and judges are really nice to kids and they try to make it easy. Keep telling your parents what your wishes are regarding custody.

What is ❓ custody?

Laura: Custody is when you will go with one parent and may not see the other as much. Or in my case you'll see one parent one day and the other parent the next—that's called "joint custody."

Marie: Custody means who is your legal guardian/caretaker. This is decided by a judge in court. The judge will decide who can take care of you best. It doesn't mean that the other parent doesn't love you or wouldn't take care of you well. It just means that, at this time, this judge thinks one parent would be a better choice. Many times the judge says it is equal and so there is joint custody. Your parents then decide when you will spend time with each of them and how much time you will spend.

"I remember when my parents first decided to separate. I wasn't sure what was happening. I could hear them fighting about who was going to get what. That confused me. I thought, 'How can it matter who gets what? We all share.' But then I saw that my parents weren't sharing much anymore. I remember opening the refrigerator and seeing little round orange stickers on the food. I couldn't imagine what they were for, until my mom asked me to grab her a Diet Coke. I brought one to her that had an orange sticker and she told me to put it back because it belonged to my dad. I laughed a little, but by the time I got to the refrigerator I was crying. I couldn't help but wonder if orange stickers were going to end up on me and my sisters."
—Marie

Why can't I live ❓ with both parents?

Laura: Because they're not going to live with each other. I was little when my parents got divorced. When my mom got remarried, I asked if my dad could live with her and her new husband! I didn't realize then that they had important reasons for living apart.

Ellen: This is the hardest part of divorce. You didn't want to divorce either of your parents, but you have to end up living with one and not the other. You can maintain a close relationship with people you don't live with. Think about it—you don't live with your best friend and you probably don't live with your grandparents. You can stay close to the parent you don't live with by talking on the phone, writing letters (even if they live close) and visiting regularly. Remind the parent who doesn't have custody that you want time to just talk, that you don't always have to do something.

Marie: Maybe you can. We do. We have bedrooms at both homes and spend half our time at one and half our time at the other. The best part is that our mom is remarried, so there are three parents. That means there is always someone available to talk, drive us somewhere or help with homework. For some parents, it takes time to get to this point, though.

Who can I talk to about the divorce?

Laura: Your mom and dad. They want to know what you think and how you feel.

Ellen: Talking to someone is good. It would be great if you had someone to talk to who you know would not take sides, like a pastor or rabbi, a teacher, club leader or a parent of a friend.

What can I do to let out some of this negative energy?

Laura: Talk to your parents, but also talk to grandparents, aunts, uncles and grown-up friends. Try to focus on good things.

Ellen: I like to write down my feelings, both good things and bad things. Sometimes I even write down what I think is going to happen. It's really interesting to look back on my predictions. I see things from a different perspective then, and I realize that even if my worst fear was true, I made it through.

Marie: Relax, meditate, take a nap, get exercise, write in your diary. Do something that uses the energy or focuses it elsewhere. Make sure you are eating and sleeping well and getting plenty of exercise. We're all crankier when we don't. Remember, fighting and yelling don't get rid of negative energy, they make it worse.

Do my mom and dad hate each other?

Laura: Maybe they do and maybe they don't hate each other. Probably they're just mad. But remember, they don't hate you.

Ellen: I doubt that they hate each other. It just seems like it because there is so much for them to disagree about right now. They are sad, though, and under a lot of stress.

Marie: In some ways they may hate each other. They can't stand living with each other and they no longer love each other the way they used to. One parent was first to realize this and decide that a divorce would be a good idea. It is the other parent who is probably the maddest and they may have some hate. Eventually, they will grow out of it.

What is a stepparent?

Laura: A stepparent is a person your mom or dad decides to marry after the divorce.

Marie: A stepparent is a parent, but not your biological/real parent. Your mom's second husband or your dad's second wife. They may already have kids of their own and those kids will become your stepsisters or stepbrothers. If your mom or dad has a child with your stepparent, that child is your half-sister or half-brother.

Do I really have to listen to my stepparent, even though they're not my real parent?

Ellen: Yes, you should listen to people who are in charge of you. Stepparents are also in charge of us. That can be good. They will have new ways to look at things and they may even have ideas and talents that neither of your parents have. They will care about you because you're the child of someone they love. They will eventually love you, too.

Marie: It's hard to take orders from someone you hardly know, and it's even harder when the person is taking a parent's time away from you.

You're probably not going to be crazy about this person at first, but everyone deserves a chance. Respect your parent by respecting their new spouse and do what is asked of you. If you think it's wrong or if you think they talk to you disrespectfully, let your parent know. But do it calmly. Temper tantrums just make everything worse.

What do I do when my divorced parents both come to a school event and fight?

Laura: Tell them how you feel. Maybe they don't realize how they look to other people and how they make you feel.

Ellen: Ask them if they can make time to work out their differences privately so that special events can stay special.

Marie: How embarrassing! If there is a way to divide up the special event, do it. Maybe one parent goes to the concert one night and the other goes the other night. Or maybe one parent goes to the first hour of the open-house and the other parent goes to the second hour. Tell your parents that their fighting is hard on you and suggest such divisions.

What can I do to get my mind off of the divorce?

Laura: You can play with friends, toys and games, or you can read and draw. Remind yourself that everything is going to be okay.

Ellen: Reading a good book always helps. A fiction book can help you escape and a non-fiction book can help you see important things going on around you—things you can get involved in and learn more about.

Marie: Do something you enjoy doing. Do something relaxing and healthy, but remember you can't escape the confusion and pain. You're going to have to experience it, but it will make you smarter and more sensitive.

My friend's parents are getting divorced. What can I do to help her?

Laura: Spend time listening to her. She is confused and has a lot to share. Her parents may not have a lot of time right now to listen to her.

Ellen: Encourage your friend by telling her that everything will be okay in the long run and that the short run will be over soon. Give her a copy of this book.

Marie: Be there for your friend. Don't take one parent's side and encourage her not to as well. She loves both of her parents and both of her parents love her. Remind her of that.

"Always remember, your parents are divorcing each other, not you. They will always love you."—Ellen

What to Do
on Those Boring Days

Emily Jung-Miller, age 12

✂ Hobbies: *collecting coins, writing, painting* ✎ Favorite class: *Gym* ☻ Pet peeve: *how life always seems to get in my way* ✿ Dream: *to grow up, be happy and not confused about anything*

I am an arts-and-crafts person and have fun doing projects like origami and miniatures. Every day I hear stories at school about how people got bored, so they started smoking or robbing. These things may sound more exciting than folding paper, but once you get into it and finish a project, you feel good, and it's a lot better for you. The games are really fun with your friends, and they become a mutual bonding experience. I thought that it would be good for girls to have a place to go when they feel like creating something but don't know how.

Origami  Cards

Materials: white 8.5" x 11" (22 x 28 cm) paper, origami paper, white glue, book of instructions, pens

Instructions: Fold the white paper from the top lengthwise to the bottom, then again from left to right. You should come up with a rectangle about 3" x 4" (7.5 x 10 cm). Design a scene you can make from the origami book, such as a boat, clouds and trees, or come up with your own design. Then make them and paste them onto the paper using a thin layer of glue. Make sure the edge with no opening is at the top. Let dry, then open your card and write something on the inside if you want.

Collage  Boxes

Materials: shells, rocks, flowers or plants of all sizes and types, a jewelry box, strong glue, sealant or lacquer

Instructions: Without gluing, arrange the shells, rocks or plants in an attractive pattern on the box top. Be sure not to use the bottom or the box will be unstable. Trace lightly around them so you can remember where they went. Then, if you're using shells or rocks, glue the bottoms to the box with hot or other strong glue. Use the glue sparingly. If you want to use plants, press them first, then white glue should be enough. If you want, brush or spray on a coat of lacquer.

Decoupage  Boxes

Materials: one to three glossy magazine pages, scissors, a pencil, a jewelry box, glue, lacquer

Instructions: Plan a design of different paper shapes with light pencil on the box. (Hint: geometric shapes look best.) Cut the magazine pages into those shapes and glue them down, following the pencil drawing. Try not to put two pieces from the same page next to each other. If you want, cover the entire box with decoupage. Let it dry, then brush or spray on up to six layers of lacquer.

Nail Art

Materials: nail polish in at least two different colors, nail decals, tiny brushes (smaller than nail brushes), a friend

Instructions: Have your friend paint your nails half one color and half another. Put on decals or paint tiny squiggles or scenes with the tiny brushes. Then you do hers!

Pom-Pom 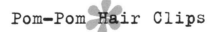 Hair Clips

Materials: plain hair clips (craft store), small pom-poms, craft eyes, hot glue

Instructions: Glue two craft eyes onto a pom-pom with small beads of glue, then glue the pom-pom onto a clip. If you want you can decorate further, but make sure you glue the decorations on securely or they might fall off.

Clay  Clips

Materials: plain hair clips (craft store), Fimo™ or Sculpey of different colors, hot glue, craft eyes, feathers, buttons or other small decorations
Instructions: Make a clay animal or object and bake it. If wanted, glue on eyes, feathers, buttons, etc. Glue the finished animal or object onto a hair clip with hot glue.

Fimo Cane Holders

Materials: Fimo of different colors, a small candle
Instructions: Make a clay animal, object or millefiori lump and let it set for two hours or bake for three minutes (until slightly firm). Stick the candle into the top of the clay object, take it back out again and widen the opening a little. Make sure it's stable, then bake the clay, and use it over and over again. By the same method, you can also make an incense holder.

Fimo Picture Frames

Materials: Fimo of different colors, a picture, a simple picture frame, glue
Instructions: Mold the Fimo over the front of the picture frame, designing how it will look. When you have it just as you want it, take it off the frame and bake it. Then glue it to the frame.

Homemade Headband or Purse

Materials: a headband or small, plain cloth purse, sequins or beads, glue/thread and needle
Instructions: For a headband, glue the sequins individually onto the headband with hot glue or spread a thin layer of tacky glue and press seed beads in patterns into it. Don't let any glue show through.

For a purse, sew beads on (use larger beads) or glue/sew sequins on. You can leave the straps plain or make them beaded, too. Either way, you have saved more than $15 on almost the exact same purse I saw in a store for $25.00.

Shell Creatures

Materials: large and small shells (in baskets at craft stores), glue, yarn, craft eyes, feathers, buttons, etc.

Instructions: Figure out how to fit the shells together to make your animal, then glue them to each other. Add eyes, buttons, lace, cloth, yarn or anything else you need to complete your project. You can use small cowry shells for ears or small overlapping scallop shells for scales. Shake it to make sure it won't come apart easily—then you're done!

Singing Contest

Materials: you, your friends, a tape recorder (optional)

Instructions: Pick a song everyone knows and likes, then have everyone sing part of it. Record them if you want to, then play it back and see who sounded best.

Fashion  Show

Materials: you, your friends, your mom or dad's old clothes

Instructions: Take the clothes and make them into themes, such as "Old West" or "'60s-style." One of you is an announcer, one or two are models and the rest are the audience. When the model comes out with the outfit on, the announcer should describe it to the audience as if they were blind. The announcer should then give a price, and audience members can try to buy it. Repeat this process for each outfit.

Produce  a Play

Materials: you, your friends, paper and pens, various props

Instructions: Think of an idea for a story. Then convert it into conversation. Pick characters and parts. Then collect props from around the house or make your own. Paint scenery or draw it on large paper. Make and borrow costumes. Rehearse the play until everybody has their lines down pat. Then, send flyers out into the neighborhood (or just to your family and friends).

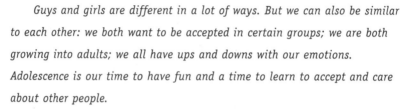

Figuring Out Guys

Tawnya Durand, age 15

✂ Hobbies: *reading, writing, acting, kayaking, hiking, running, dancing, singing, skiing, salmon fishing* 📖 Favorite writer: *Laura Ingalls Wilder* ☹ Pet peeve: *dirty socks on a couch* ❀ Dreams: *to have an exciting and enjoyable life; to be in the Iditarod, a dogsled race. I would also like to learn to sail.*

Guys and girls are different in a lot of ways. But we can also be similar to each other: we both want to be accepted in certain groups; we are both growing into adults; we all have ups and downs with our emotions. Adolescence is our time to have fun and a time to learn to accept and care about other people.

Guys are an important topic for an advice book for girls, because so many girls are trying to understand them. The advice given in this chapter is hopefully advice that will help you make good decisions or help girls and guys have fun in a safe and healthy way.

Is it love or a crush?

A crush is when you feel as if you are falling head over heels for a person. It usually only lasts for a few days or weeks.

Love is a deeper feeling you get when you care a lot about someone. Love lasts longer than a crush—months or even years. If you follow your heart and have patience you'll know if it's love or not. Give yourself lots of time to figure it out.

What's the right age to start dating?

In America many different cultures come together. Each culture has a different view on how guys and girls should act around each other about when and how they should date.

Many of the families that recently immigrated to America will have the same views on dating and relationships as the culture they came from. Families that have roots in another country, but have been in America several generations will most likely go by American ways of thinking when it comes to dating.

These different beliefs about dating aren't wrong, they're just different. Some parents don't care what age their children start dating, but set curfews for when their kids should be home. Other parents don't let their children date until they are a certain age. Some girls prefer to wait to date, while others don't. When you start dating depends on when you feel comfortable with it and when your family feels comfortable with it. You all may need to compromise a little. But the most important thing to know is that dating is a way to get to know a guy and to help learn about how to care about others.

Great Places For A First Date

- A funny movie is a terrific way to hit it off with your date.
- Lunch or dinner at a local pizza place can be fun.
- A cute cafe for hot cocoa and deli sandwiches is romantic, and my personal favorite.
- Ice skating in the winter is great as long as you dress warmly.
- Swimming at a water hole or pool can be fun in the summer.
- If you and your date are athletic, you could go for a run, hike or bike ride together.
- A barbecue with a group of friends is always exciting.
- A study date makes you smarter, and you enjoy yourself.
- If a fair or carnival comes to your town, this could be a perfect date. But make sure not to eat a lot before going on twirly rides.

Can I handle a long-distance relationship?

A long-distance relationship is when you keep contact with someone who lives far away. Let's say you went on a vacation and met a guy and went out with him a couple of times. Before you left to go home, you and that guy agreed to be boyfriend and girlfriend and hoped to see each other again sometime. That's the beginning of a long-distance relationship.

Long-distance relationships are really hard to keep going. For the most part, you are never sure if you will see the person again. Also, people change. Long-distance relationships are possible, but they're not easy. Letters, phone calls, and e-mail are okay, but you soon realize that it's very different from seeing each other and getting to know each other in person.

Is it okay to just be friends with a guy?

It's all right to be only friends with a guy. Guys and girls do not always have to be boyfriend and girlfriend. If you feel pressure from a guy to be more than friends when you just want to be friends, you need to tell him how you feel and make sure he understands that you only want to be friends.

If you like a guy a lot and he only wants to be friends, then you need to respect him. If you try to force the relationship to be more, you will most likely lose his friendship. Remember, it is better to be friends than nothing at all.

And of course, one of the very best ways to start a relationship with someone you want to be going out with is by being friends first. Give it lots of time to develop.

What if my best friend starts dating before me and I feel left out?

Your best friend has a new boyfriend, and whenever you are around her and her guy, you just don't feel comfortable. After a while your best friend doesn't seem to have any time to spend with you. You feel left out and a little bit jealous.

Here's what you can do to get this friendship back:

1. Call your best friend and tell her how you feel. She might not have realized that you were feeling left out.

2. Make plans to do some fun stuff with your friend, without her boyfriend. The two of you could go swimming or hiking or whatever you both enjoy. It's important to spend one-on-one girl time together, even when guys come into your lives.

3. If #1 and #2 don't work, spend time getting to know your other friends you might not hang out with as much. Most likely, you and your best friend will eventually connect again.

Remember, even if you don't have a boyfriend and your friend does, it's not a big deal. Your time will come. Never feel like you have to rush into things to be like someone else.

What if my boyfriend and I don't have time for each other?

Claire and Ted had a great relationship. They had a lot in common and everyone thought they were a terrific match. The problem was that Claire was busy with soccer, and Ted's parents wanted him to spend more time at home. It was really hard for Ted and Claire to find time for each other, so eventually they decided to be "just friends," but neither was happy about that decision.

It's obvious Ted and Claire care a lot about each other. If both of them want the relationship to start again, they should have another talk. They should find out how they really feel about each other (Do they both care about each other equally, or does one person want the relationship more than the other?). If they do feel the same way about each other, maybe they could set aside time for each other every week. Ted could even go to some of Claire's soccer games.

Great Gifts for Guys

When you pick out a gift for a guy you will probably want to make

sure it is something he will like, so keep his interests in mind.

Some Ideas:

- Anything that has food or candy in it will be liked.
- CDs are an easy gift to pick out.
- A cool tee-shirt is a fun gift.
- My dad likes ties and good books.
- Plan something you can do together.

Will guys still like me if I express my real opinions and act like who I truly am?

How guys feel about open-minded girls completely depends on the guy. If a guy accepts himself and has a lot of acceptance for other people, he should have no problem accepting the opinions of a girl. If a guy does not have a lot of self-acceptance, he might be reluctant to accept different ideas than what he believes. He might not listen to you, and he might even make fun of you.

Don't forget: guys are just people, so don't worry too much about how you act around them. Just be true to yourself and act the way you normally do. Everything will fall into place, and you'll eventually meet the right guy for you, if you like who you are.

76

The Friend Ship

Alissa L. Greenberg, age 10

✂ Hobbies: *writing stories and poems, reading, playing piano and viola, horseback riding, swimming* 📖 Favorite writer: *Roald Dahl* ☹ Pet peeve: *people continuously nagging me* ❋ Dream: *to be an author/illustrator with my own book published by the age of 17*

Friendship is important to me in many ways. Friends are there for me when I am feeling down or lonely and there to have fun with me and brighten my life. Friendship is also important because it gives me confidence and makes me feel good to know that I am special enough to have friends. Friendship doesn't always make me feel good, though. It has ups and downs—the downs being jealousy, meanness and so on. That's why I decided to write this chapter—to give girls advice on the highs and lows of friendship.

Friendship is very much like the ocean. On your voyage, you may encounter seaweed and dangerous rocky waters; you will meet true friends who are like ships on the sea and not-so-good friends who are like an undertow. When the waters are choppy, I hope you'll consult this chapter for help.

Making Friends: The Voyage Begins

Here are a few suggestions on how to make friends. If you are shy, people might mistake your quietness for "I'm better than you, so I won't talk to you." You'll end up with a reputation as a snob and have few friends. It's a hard process, but try to overcome your shyness. Find out where kids in your area hang out—the skating rink, movie theater, a club, etc. Go there and try to get to know people. Be nice to everybody and don't be judgmental. If everyone is nasty to someone, don't be nasty too, just to be cool. Instead, try to make friends with that person. Hey, he or she could be nice!!! If you're non-judgmental, honest and nice, you should set sail on the Friend Ship in no time.

How to Tell if Your New Friend Ship Will Be "Smooth Sailing"

If you have a new friend, you'll probably be curious about what kind of "ship" she is. One way to get the answer is to watch her with her other friends. Is she mean sometimes and nice at others? Then she is probably a "Lighthouse Friend." Does she talk about friends behind their backs? Then she is probably a "Pirate Friend." It is up to you to decide if she has the right kind of nature to be *your* friend—will you sail well together?

Pirate Friend or Not? Will She Be a True Friend?

A Pirate Friend is not a friend at all. She is someone who acts like your friend, but really just wants to steal your happiness and possibly your other friends. She will ambush you when you least expect it. Although they may act like it up front, Pirate Friends are usually *not*: very kind, willing to share, able to keep secrets, loyal, fun or honest.

Try to detect a Pirate Friend before it is too late, or you could end up with major-league hurt feelings.

Lighthouse Friends: How to Survive Them

A Lighthouse Friend is a person who is sometimes nice to you and sheds her "light" on you, but is sometimes mean and leaves you in her "shadow." Although friends like these can be very nice at times, they are unpredictable and therefore undependable. You need to be prepared for the "shadow" times. If you have a Lighthouse Friend, then you should make sure that you have lots of other good friends to support you and have fun with you until you see the light again.

Be patient, because a lot of times a Lighthouse Friend will change into a real friend when she becomes more secure about you and more understanding of how friendship works.

Sea Urchin Friends

A sea urchin is a round shellfish covered in spiny prickles, which make it look very tough, like it could handle anything. However, when you pick it up the prickles fall off, and you find it is quite fragile underneath. Sea Urchin Friends come in with a "don't-mess-with-me" attitude, but the moment kids pick on them, they become shy and their feelings get hurt easily. You should watch out for Sea Urchin Friends—not so you can defend yourself against them, but so that you can protect their shells from breaking. If a Sea Urchin Friend is being picked on, stand up for her. After all, you know her secret. And if she gives you her prickly side, be patient. She's just trying to defend her soft side from getting hurt.

If Waters Get Rocky

One of the most common problems in friendship is getting into arguments. You could be arguing with a friend or you could be caught in the middle of someone else's fight. Arguments can be about things as complicated as boys or as simple as what station to watch on TV! If you're in a fight, lean on your other friends until waters get smoother. Keep yourself busy so that you can forget the argument. Go to the movies, read a book—anything to keep from focusing too much on it.

Completely keeping out of arguments is almost impossible, but you can devise a system with your friends so that you won't fight so much. Here are some ideas:

• Whenever one person wants to do one thing and another person wants to do something else, it would be one person's turn to win the disagreement. The next time, the other person gets his or her way.

• Make an argument spinner with everyone's name on it. One person spins and the person whose name comes up wins the argument. Be creative. Something totally wacky may stop the fights!

Do you often get stuck in the middle of your friends' fights with each other? Here's some advice:

• Don't help them fight. If one friend comes up to you and insults another friend behind his or her back, don't spread the mean gossip to that other friend. Just stay out of it totally.

• You might start to worry, "Will they force me to take sides?" Avoid this by hanging out somewhere else with other people. You don't have to ignore your fighting friends, but staying away from them a little reduces the danger of them making you take sides. Usually, their fight will be over before you know it, and everyone will be friends again.

The Green-Eyed Monster of the Deep

Are you jealous that your friend is prettier than you or that another friend is better at sports? Whatever the reason, there is one thing that you almost definitely need to do and that is to stop being so competitive. It may be hard, but try.

Stop concentrating on what other people can do and focus on what you are good at. Try to get better in the areas you want to improve. Most of the time the jealousy will go away. You might even notice that your deck is cleaner and you are steering straighter. Hopefully, the Green-Eyed Monster named Jealousy will never catch you again.

Avoiding the Undertow

Do you have a friend who's constantly on your back to do something and telling you you're a chicken if you don't? If so, you are experiencing peer pressure. Peer pressure is like an undertow. You can escape the undertow by forcing yourself out of its current. Walk away to get some space for yourself so that you can think clearly. If the undertow is still there when you come back and you still don't want to be sucked in, another escape is to distract them with something fun you know they'll want to do. Later, out of the pull of the undertow, really think hard, "Do I want to do what these kids are bugging me to? What can I lose if I say 'no' and what will happen if I say 'yes'?" Answer yourself honestly. Will it sink your ship? You decide.

When the Gulls Squawk About You

It is a very painful experience to have "Gulls" squawking about you behind your back. It is especially painful when you used to think of those Gulls as friends. Think of why the Gulls might be talking about you. Are they jealous? Did you do something to them? If you find a real reason, don't approach the Gulls immediately. If they had a real reason to squawk, then you know it probably won't happen again if you don't do what bothered them in the first place.

If the squawking continues or if they have no good reason, confront them. Ask them why they did it. Tell them you were hurt because they talked behind your back and you don't think it was fair. Tell them that in the future they should tell you directly when they have a problem, and you can work it out *together*. Then go on with your life.

Calming the Storm

Did you and your friend get in a fight? You know that you and she both want to make up? Well, it's time for you to take action. Apologizing is a very tough process, but it pays off. First of all, go up to your friend and ask her to forgive you. Say that no one is perfect. Then (here's the hard part) admit what you did wrong and apologize. This is easier said than done, but remember, it pays off. Chances are she'll do the same.

Helping Friends Survive Stormy Seas

Does your friend have lots of problems? Does she usually pour her heart out about them to you? Well, you are not alone. Lots of kids experience this. Your friend is going through some "stormy seas" and needs help "steering." Here's what to do to help her.

If your friend asks you for advice on something, think hard about it. Dig deep into your heart and try to figure out what you would do. You could even consult this book and see if there is advice for your friend's problem in it. Listen a lot. Answer her questions as truthfully as possible and hopefully, over time the problems will end. If they get worse, not better, you might consider asking advice from a teacher, parent or guidance counselor.

When the Tide Goes Out on Your Friendship

Have you stopped liking a friend? Is she mean to you? Sometimes you just have to let go. Say you and another girl have been friends ever since kindergarten, but now things are changing. She doesn't like the same things as you and maybe she's even being mean to you to impress other friends. What can you do? Hang out with other kids. Go to events without her. You'll communicate less and less, but when you do talk, try not to have cross words. In time, the friendship will probably break up, but that doesn't mean you have to be enemies. You can drift apart from a friend without fighting in the process.

Sometimes, when the tide goes out, you can get stuck in some seaweed. This happens when you have a friend you are just not interested in anymore, but you don't want to leave her because she doesn't have any other friends. It seems that no matter what you do to separate from the relationship, you just become more entangled. Here's some advice:

1. Make sure you really want to separate from your friend.

2. If you are sure, slowly drift away. Don't spend as much time with her, and hang out with other kids more. Gradually she'll make new friends and it won't be so painful for her to lose you.

3. If she's getting teased in school, you should stand up for her. After all, you should still be nice to people who aren't "ships" for you.

As you can see, it is challenging to sail the "Friend Ship," but it certainly is worth it. Bon Voyage!

Best Friend Projects

Abigayle Schmidt, age 12

✄ Hobbies: *reading, playing with my pets* ✎ Favorite class: *Science* 📖 Favorite book: The Chronicles of Narnia ☹ Pet peeve: *people spelling my name wrong* ♬ Heroes: *Amelia Earhart and my mom, because she works so hard* ❀ Dream: *to be a chemist and create cures for deadly diseases*

Do you like to have fun with your friends? If so, you've turned to the right page. In this chapter you will find activities to do with your best friend. These activities have been tested by my best friend and myself, so trust me, they're great! After you complete them, you can save them and they'll always remind you of the fun you had making them and of your friendship. So enough talking—let's get crafty!

The Friendship Box

A friendship box is a place where you and your best friend can keep your memories—notes, photos and other momentos from your special friendship. I suggest you keep your box under or beside your bed. Whenever your best friend comes over, you'll have another chance to add to it!

Materials: 2 shoe boxes, ribbon, markers, tape, wrapping paper, scissors and stickers

Instructions:
1. Cover each box with wrapping paper.
2. Cut two pieces of ribbon to the same length. [Approx. 2 ft. (60 cm)]
3. Use a pencil to punch a hole at each end of the boxes. Stick a ribbon end through each hole and tie knots inside the box so the ribbon can't slip through. This will be your shoulder strap.

4. Write your names on each of the boxes with the marker.

5. Decorate the boxes with the stickers or use decoupage (see the "What to Do on Those Boring Days" chapter). Be creative!

Seashell  Frames

These picture frames can hold pictures of you and your best friend. You can put them in your friendship boxes or on your nightstands. And if your friend moves, you'll have something to remember each other by.

Materials: 24 Popsicle sticks, 2 seashells, glue, 2 3- x 4-in. (7.5- x 10-cm) pictures of you and your friend

Instructions:

1. Glue 10 Popsicle sticks together side by side to make a "raft." Repeat this with another 10 sticks. You should now have 2 rafts.

2. Glue a stick across the top and bottom of each "raft".

3. Now glue a picture in the middle of each one.

4. Finally, glue a shell in one corner of each frame for a decorative touch. You may also want to use other materials to decorate the frames. Create your own unique style!

Locker Bulletin Board

This bulletin board will be very helpful and it will also be fun! You can put it in your locker and pin up all of the notes, photos, etc. that you and your friend share. I use it not only to hold notes and photos, but also to remind me of class projects.

Materials: a 5- x 5-in. (12.5- x 12.5-cm) piece of cardboard, glue, a 6- x 6-in. (15- x 15-cm) piece of cloth, a 1- x 5-in. (2.5- x 12.5-cm) piece of sticky-back magnet

Instructions:

1. Glue the cloth over the cardboard, covering the front of it completely.

2. Stick the magnet to the back of the cardboard.

3. Put the bulletin board in your locker, on your refrigerator or on any other metal surface.

Best Friend  Biography

This project will show you how to create a short biography about you and your best friend.

Materials: 1 large piece of construction paper, snapshots of you and your friend, notes or other momentos, glue, pencils and scissors

Instructions:

1. Fold the paper so that the side edges meet in the middle, like a big card.

2. Glue the snapshots along each side of the center fold.

3. On each side, beside the pictures of yourself and your friend, write each other's biography. Be sure to write about all the ways your friend is special to you and about the fun things you enjoy doing together.

New Kid on the Block

Christina Meyer, age 13

🏹 Hobbies: *model rocketry, writing, knitting, playing piano*

🐚 Favorite class: *Science* 📖 Favorite book: *My Friend Flicka*

☹ Pet peeve: *when girls my age do nothing but giggle, gossip and talk on the phone* 📖 Hero: *Eleanor Roosevelt*

❀ Dream: *to become the best writer I can be*

Mariana Meyer, age 11

🏹 Hobbies: *playing clarinet and piano, reading*

📖 Favorite writer: *Isaac Asimov* ☹ Pet peeve: *when people interrupt my reading or my privacy* 📖 Hero: *Rosa Parks*

❀ Dreams: *to be a veterinarian and to find a cure for cancer*

We chose this topic because we wanted to give advice to other girls who are making changes. When we started writing, we were in the middle of a big change ourselves—switching schools. Nobody likes being the new kid on the block. It can be frightening, intimidating and downright depressing. The good news is that you're not alone. Everyone has to be the new kid at some point—new school, new job, going to camp, going to college—and you will be okay. It may not happen overnight and it may not always be fun. But, it will be okay. On the other side of things, some people don't know how to act around a new kid. Our chapter will help new kids feel included and help other kids know how to treat them.

How do I make new friends?

Christina: Making friends isn't something that happens overnight. Don't rush it. I find it best if you're subtly outgoing. Don't intrude on people, but try to be the first one to start a friendship. Help someone pick up their books or help them study. Ask the girl across the street if she wants to jump rope. Show that you're a nice person: be a good listener and be genuinely interested. Give compliments. Don't be too pushy—most kids don't like it when others show off, interrupt or give too much negative criticism.

You can also join clubs, play on a sports team or join the school band at the new place. You'll not only meet people who have a common interest, but you'll work together with them. I made friends at my new school through being in classes together, having a nearby locker and singing in chorus. There are lots of ways to make friends, and there's sure to be someone out there who's willing to make a new pal!

Mariana: I agree that making friends doesn't happen quickly, but I get friends in a different way. I am friendly to people who come to me first. People who are nice enough to approach me are likely to make good friends. Then, often I meet their friends and so on. (You be the judge of which approach works for you.)

One key tip in meeting new people is to remember your values. Don't force yourself to interact with people whose activities or interests you are not comfortable with. You might be tempted to do things you might not other-wise do just to "fit in" or make friends—but don't. It's not worth it. Sooner or later, you'll meet kids who share your interests and who you'll be comfort-able with. That's what friendship is all about!

How do I show people what I'm really like?

Christina: Be yourself and show your sense of humor. Smile a lot—this makes people feel comfortable around you, and soon they might get to know you better. Work hard at the things that you do well; people will start to notice your talents and you'll achieve welcome recognition.

Don't be afraid to show what you can do, but don't strut it in front of everyone. Shortly after starting at my new school, I was assigned to perform an experiment for my Science class. I had worked with model rockets for several years, and after struggling to find a good experiment, I decided to bring my rockets into class. I explained how they worked and launched a rocket outside for my classmates. It was a great conversation starter! Everyone thought it was really cool.

Mariana: Don't hold back your opinions—speak them out. You don't need to be a show-off or overbearing, but do share your thoughts. Don't be afraid to say what you think!

How do I leave my previous "comfort zone"?

Christina: You don't have to. You'll always have memories of the fun you had at the old place. Write a story about it or look at pictures to relive those memories. Sometimes I still call the girls at my old school. Also, think about the positive aspects of being new—nobody at the new place knows your most embarrassing moments or old mistakes. This is your chance to make a fresh start.

Mariana: Keep in touch. Call up old friends, visit, arrange fun activities together. You're not necessarily separated for life. Even if you're far away, in another state or even another country, you still can write. Everyone loves to get a letter. If you're feeling really depressed, have a good cry and talk to someone about it. It makes you feel better after you let it all out.

What if someone makes fun of me?

Christina: Though it may be hard, brush it off. You don't have to socialize with rude people. Hold firm to what you believe and don't let go. Find someone who respects you and what you believe in and be their friend. Sometimes the most critical people are those who themselves are the most insecure. That's their problem, not yours.

Mariana: I just ignore the teaser if someone makes fun of me. Other times I respond, "That's not true!" or I laugh it off. Most of the time, what they say isn't true, and often the trouble-maker is just jealous. If teasing really gets out of hand—if you feel as though you are being ganged up on or if it gets particularly nasty, talk to someone about it—a parent, your school advisor, a teacher, even a big sister or brother.

How do I tell people I haven't done something before without looking dumb?

Christina: Be truthful and tell them you haven't done whatever it is before, but that you'd love to learn and have been wanting to learn how. Decent people won't make fun of you—they will show you how.

Mariana: I agree. If people make fun of you or laugh when you say you haven't done it before, don't hang around them.

How do I find my way around?

Christina: If you can, get a map of the school or wherever you're moving. Ask for a floor plan of the school, a map of the new town or even a map of the county. "Walk" your way through the map before you go. Before I started at my new school, we had orientation. I felt hopelessly lost, so I asked for a map. At home I studied it and pretended I was walking through the hallways in the floor plan. When I started school, I found my way around very easily!

Mariana: Don't be afraid to ask for help. It's normal, and kids shouldn't blame you—you're new!

How do I deal with lunchroom trauma?

Christina: The same strategies apply: be nice, chin up, take the initiative if you have to — it ultimately will work out. On the first day at my new school, a girl invited me to sit with her at lunch. Walking into the lunchroom that day, I saw with despair that she was sitting at a full table. I had a sinking feeling that I would have to sit alone. I resolved to find a seat with someone who looked pleasant. Nervously, I looked for a table that wasn't crowded. "Chin up," I thought. "Be brave." In the midst of my mental pep talk, a girl tapped me on the shoulder and invited me to sit at her table. Rescued! I became good friends with all the girls at that table and I continue to sit with them at lunch.

Mariana: My strategy was to get to the lunchroom early. I sat at a prominent empty table, and people came and joined me. I smiled and said, "Hi!" to the girls who now have become my friends.

I'm around so many people, yet I still feel lonely.

Christina: Get interested in what others are doing and thinking. Ask questions about them, and sooner or later they'll be interested in you. Be a good listener and give compliments. Just show that you're a nice person, and people will want to be your friend. And remember, it won't happen overnight.

Mariana: It's normal. Don't pay too much attention to yourself. It's often easy to get lost in self-misery. Also, it really helps to smile a lot. It opens yourself up to people, and others feel more comfortable around you. Soon you won't feel very lonely anymore!

Sometimes I don't want to face all these new people—I just want to stay in bed.

Christina: That's a normal feeling, too. Force yourself to get out. If you're really shy, remember that other people may be just as shy as you are. One of my friends I met this year was new just like me. She told me that it helped her to know that there were other people who were nervous and shy about being new, too.

Mariana: Think about it. If you don't experience change in your life, it's going to be boring. Go out and meet new people. If you stay in bed, you're never going to make friends.

What if I don't like the change?

Christina: Don't dwell on the bad points. That will only make you more depressed. Figure out what makes you happy about whatever is new and focus on that. Though you may see nothing good about it now, once you get to know people and get the hang of things, it will become bearable and then enjoyable.

Mariana: Everyone resists change, but I agree that you should focus on the good aspects of any change. There has to be something positive about it. Maybe your mom or dad got a new job and had to move. Although you may feel stepped on, the new job could mean more opportunities for your family.

How should I treat someone new?

Christina: Everybody loves to see a friendly face, especially when they're new. Ask the new girl to sit with you at lunch. Offer to show her around. Introduce her to your friends. Talk with her and get to know her better. You'll get a taste of her personality. You might find you have a lot in common and you'll have made two people happy.

Mariana: It always is nice to be welcomed by a smile. Or at least try not to be too grumpy. You don't want to make the new kid even more depressed. Call a new girl just to check in. Ask if everything is going all right or if you can help out in any way. Invite her over. You'll make a new friend and the new kid will feel great. Whether at school or elsewhere, be a nice host—show the new kid around and don't treat her like a trespasser. Put yourself in her shoes and think about what you would like if you were in that situation.

To Sum Up

Difficult as it may be, we think being new actually gives us interesting opportunities. It's a new start. If you're new, no one really knows what you're like, who you are or what you are capable of. If you have made mistakes in the past, now they are really in the past.

Being new can give you an opportunity to shine. Take the opportunity and run with it!

Unlocking the Writer Inside You

Katie Hedberg, age 11

✂ Hobbies: *biking, swimming, softball, volleyball, singing, soccer, piano, trumpet, cross-stitching, cooking, reading, Girl Scouts, writing* 📖 Favorite writer: *Mary Downing Hanne* ☹ Pet peeve: *when boys act like I'm stupid* ♙ Hero: *my mom* ✿ Dream: *to become a professional writer of mysteries, children's stories and fiction*

I have always loved to write. I started to write years ago, mostly fiction and poems. I also keep a diary, which helps me sort out my thoughts and feelings and is a source of ideas. Because I write so much, I know a few things about writing, such as ideas and tools you need. This chapter should be good for all you girls who want to become writers one day; it will give you some pointers to help you start writing.

How Can I Get in the "Writing Mood"?

Reading: Reading is very important! It helps stretch your mind and gives you ideas about how your favorite authors wrote their stories. It also gets you ready to write your story.

Research: This helps if you are writing non-fiction, historical fiction or science fiction. You should do research at the library, at school or on the Internet (if you have access to it). Look around for cool information and take notes, because for sure, you will not remember what you learned. After each paragraph you read, ask yourself, "Are there any main ideas I should write down?" Then you should make an outline of the things you want to add in your writing.

Music: Listen to music, so that you can get relaxed and in the mood for writing. It could also help inspire you, depending on the kind of music and the type of story you want to write. Say you wanted to write a story about a woman who believed in God—you could listen to a band that sings about God.

Brainstorm: First, totally relax and clear your mind. Then write down anything that pops into your head. From this list, choose an idea to write about. Once you've chosen an idea, brainstorm for details that you want to include. Now you're ready to write!

What's the Best Time & Place For Writing?

The environment you're in while you write is very important. What works best for you may be different from me, so here are some ideas:

Where to write: My dad likes to write in his office and my sister likes to write on her bed. My teacher likes to write in her den and her living room. Ann M. Martin, author of *The Babysitters Club*, likes to write in a little room in her apartment. I like to write at my desk or in the dining room. Other people might like to write outside or in a library.

When to write: You can write anytime. I like to write in the afternoon or the evening, but morning can be a calm and quiet time to write, too (on weekends, at least). Many people feel they can concentrate best on their writing when they're alone and when other things aren't demanding their time.

What Tools Do I Need?

Here's a list of things you should have when you write to help you write a better and richer story.

The Dictionary: There are two reasons why I think a dictionary is important. First, have you ever heard your mom, dad, brother, sister, etc. say a word that you thought would be cool to use in your story? The only problem is, you don't have a clue what it means. That's when you can use the dictionary to look it up. Second, have you ever felt bored with adding onto your story? I have, but I flipped through my dictionary and found cool words that I never knew existed!

The Thesaurus: A thesaurus is a book of words and their synonyms (words that basically mean the same thing). Have you ever gotten stuck on a story because you couldn't find the right word to use? For example, you want to use a word that means "good," but not the word "good" itself. With a thesaurus you would find words such as "decent," "proper" and "appropriate."

Something to Write With: A pen will work, but a pencil is nicer because you can erase and rewrite things. You'll also need a piece of paper or a notebook. Some people prefer notebooks because you can keep your whole story together. Other writers like to write on a computer, which definitely has its advantages. A computer usually has a built-in speller and the-saurus, and you can go back to parts of your story easily.

What Kind of Writing Should I Do?

You may ask yourself, "What should I write?" There is no "right" kind of writing. I recommend you try different kinds to see which one you like best. Some writers stick to one style, but others, like me, enjoy all different kinds of writing. Here are some kinds of writing that you could try:

• Journalism—the kind of writing you do when you work at a newspaper. You write just the facts of the story.

• Editorials—you write an essay of your opinions (like a letter to the editor in a newspaper).

• Poems—shorter writing that usually rhymes, but not always.

• Plays—stories that people act out.

• Non-fiction—writing about a subject that is real or true.

• Fiction—a kind of story that is made up or imagined.

• Science fiction—fiction that is based on scientific phenomena, like space travel or nuclear weapons.

• Historical fiction—fiction based on things that happened in the past.

Where Do I Get Ideas for Stories?

* Keep a diary or journal. If you write in it regularly, you will always have ideas for stories when you flip through it.

* Think back to a time that you remember, and then you can change it a little to make it a new story.

* Go through newspapers and magazines for interesting ideas.

* Look at other stories you have written. Maybe you want to make them into a series.

* Maybe your friends or a parent or teacher will tell you something exciting they did, and you can write a story about that.

* Write about things that happened in the past. Look through a history book and put yourself in that time during some event. What would it be like?

* And don't forget to READ!! It helps develop your ideas.

How Do I Make Up Characters?

When you write a story, you almost always have characters. Where do they come from? Here are some ideas:

* Sometimes I base characters on friends I know.

* Some are totally made-up sorts of people.

* You can base characters loosely on yourself.

* Some of the techniques for coming up with story ideas apply to making up characters, too. For example, you could base characters on historical figures or on people you read about in newspapers and magazines.

Be sure your characters are true to life. The characters are made up and you want to make them perfect, but they should make mistakes like real people. It is also a good idea to give some description of a character—hair color, eye color, height, etc. Where does she come from? What is her background? What's her personality like? When you describe your characters, it helps your writing because you are able to see the characters in your mind.

How Do I Start Writing the Story?

When I write short stories, I can just start typing on the computer. With long stories, I sometimes need to make an outline.

An outline is where you take your story and lay it out into different parts. There are main topics and then under the main topics you have subtopics of what you want to include in that part of the story.

Once you have your outline, you can start your story. In a story there are three parts: the introduction, the body and the closing. The introduction is the beginning of the story where you first meet the characters and the setting. You also start to see the plot of the story. The body is where the story unfolds. Usually, there's some sort of conflict or problem that the characters are trying to solve. The closing is where you finally find out how the characters deal with the conflict or problem.

After you're done with your story, show it to someone and ask for their thoughts. Their comments can help you see the strengths and weaknesses in your story so that you can revise it and make it better.

What If I Get Writer's Block?

Have you ever had a time when you just could not write? That's writer's block. Try to stay calm and don't go into panic mode. Writer's block might make you think about quitting writing. Do not let it do that to you! Ann M. Martin, author of *The Baby-Sitters Club* series, suggests that if you get writer's block, you should do other things besides writing and should not even think about your story.

Every author gets it, so don't worry. After a few days you should go back to your story and ask yourself questions such as, "Is my story missing something?" Then think of some ways that you can make changes. Try using the brainstorm technique again. Keep working on your story!

What Is Proofreading?

When you first write a story, it won't be in perfect form. Your first copy is called your rough draft. On this you can cross out things you don't want anymore and add things you forgot. You can check your spelling with a dictionary or spell checker. You can add punctuation and details. You can see how your story is put together and then you can move its parts around. You can also check for grammatical errors like run-on sentences and subject-verb agreement.

After you're done with proofreading, ask yourself these questions. Did I:

* Indent?

* Make each sentence a complete thought?

* Use capital letters correctly?

* Use punctuation marks correctly?

* Spell all words correctly?

How Do I Get My Writing Published?

For this part, I interviewed the editor of our local newspaper, the managing editor of the magazine *New Moon,* and an editor at Beyond Words Publishing about how kids can get published.

In Newspapers: Newspapers will sometimes print non-fiction letters about a local topic that are sent in from students. They like this letter typed, and you should remember to keep it short because newspapers do not have a lot of room. Reread your letter to make sure you did not make any mistakes. Use good grammar and spelling and try as hard as you can to make it neat. Give it your best! You might also try sending in a column idea. In one newspaper, two high-school boys review local coffee shops every weekend. Think of ideas that should have a kid's perspective.

In Magazines: Most magazines take fiction, non-fiction, poetry and letters. They like to have them typed, but if you can't use a computer or typewriter, then handwrite them neatly. Each magazine takes stories of different page lengths. You can call them and ask for their "submission guidelines." Certain magazines might also have guidelines for the subject matter of stories. For example, in *New Moon,* they like stories to be about girls. Your writing should use words appropriate for the magazine's age groups. Look at some past issues of the magazine you want to submit your writing to. Figure out who you think reads the magazine and write for that group.

Getting a Book Published: Type or handwrite your book idea. If your idea needs illustrations, draw them yourself or have someone else draw them. Go to the library and get a book called *The Literary Marketplace* by R. R. Bowker, which lists all the publishers in America and the kinds of books they publish. When you've found the publishers that do books like yours, write a short letter to each editor telling her about your book and about you, and try to make her laugh. Send the letter, your manuscript, copies of your illustrations and a self-addressed stamped envelope (so they can return your stuff to you) to each publisher you picked.

Remember:

1. Have patience. It may take an editor many months to read and return your story or to call you.

2. Don't get hurt feelings if someone gives you suggestions or wants to change something about your story. Understand what they mean and realize that it's just their suggestion. One person's opinion doesn't mean that everybody else will think the same way, but often an outsider's suggestion can help make your writing even better.

3. Don't get discouraged by rejection letters. Many famous authors were rejected hundreds of times before they were first published. Have faith in yourself and keep trying. If you give up, you'll never get published!

Closing

Writing takes practice. When you write your rough draft, you might think that it's no good. Keep working on your writing until you get it the way you like. It doesn't have to be perfect the first time because no one is perfect. You'll probably enter contests with your writing, and for sure you won't win all the time. Don't get frustrated and give up. Keep trying to do your best!

If you want to learn more about writing or getting published, here are some books you can read:

A Writer's Notebook: Unlocking the Writer Within You by Ralph Fletcher

Writing with Style by Sue Young

The Young Writer's Handbook by Susan Tchudi

Edit Yourself: A Manual For Everyone Who Works With Words
by Bruce Ross-Larson

A Beginner's Guide to Getting Published by Kirk Polking

The Complete Guide to Writing Fiction by Barnaby Conrad

Here are a few ideas for magazines to send your writing to:

Stone Soup: The Magazine by Young Writers and Artists

Creative Kids: The National Voice for Kids

Merlyn's Pen: The National Magazine for Student Writing

Skipping Stones: A Multicultural Children's Magazine

New Moon: The Magazine for Girls and Their Dreams

American Girl

Strength Out of Sadness:
Teenage Depression

Heidi Schmaltz, age 14

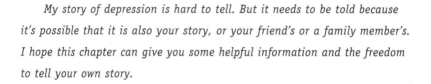

✂ Hobbies: *writing and the Girls' Movement!!* ✎ Favorite classes: *Spanish and Biology* ☹ Pet peeve: *ignorant people* ♬ Hero: *Sojourner Truth* ❀ Dream: *I want to travel everywhere!*

My story of depression is hard to tell. But it needs to be told because it's possible that it is also your story, or your friend's or a family member's. I hope this chapter can give you some helpful information and the freedom to tell your own story.

My  Story

Depression is rarely acknowledged in children. Maybe people don't think we have the ability to be truly depressed. As if we haven't been through hard enough times. Depression isn't about hard times. It's something that happens inside you, no matter what's going on in the outside world. We try to explain it as something caused by a definable thing—we wonder what and how and why and who. Because we can answer none of these, we can't accept our feelings.

As a young child I was smart, happy, unafraid to speak my mind and full of ideas. I can't recall exactly when the depression started, but I believe it was around third grade. At that time if you asked me why I felt depressed, you would've gotten a long list of little pointless things. But really, I don't know how my depression started.

In the world outside my head my parents were splitting up. Perhaps the divorce and my own loneliness contributed to the depression and to the fact that it went unnoticed.

I went off to counseling to ease the pain of the divorce. A lot of people think if you go to counseling you'll get "fixed" in four sessions, but it's not like that. You really have to work at it. After those first sessions,

I still wasn't "cured."

My depression stuck with me all the way to middle school. Just like an old dirty pair of jeans—ugly, but so comfortable to wear. The school I had enrolled in was teeming with intolerance toward anyone different, anyone troubled. They knew how to deal with the classic stereotypes: quiet, obedient girls and loud, aggressive boys. Anything else confused them. I confused them.

As a result, my visits to the "Student Management Specialist" increased while my grades dropped. Because I was already under this cloud of depression, middle school just confused me. I lived down to everyone's expectations. School to me then was sickening to the point where I suffered terrible headaches, stomach aches and claustrophobia. I always just had to get away. I went deeper into my problem.

At that time I hadn't been to counseling for a while, since the divorce issues were dealt with. One day, I told my mom I needed to go again. I didn't really know why, but I knew there was something wrong. I was scared to admit anything was seriously wrong, though. It was a while before we figured out the real problem.

During this second round of counseling, things really started to take shape. We finally figured out that I was clinically depressed, which was a huge turning point. Until then, we really didn't know the cause of my troubles. What I had was moderate depression, the most common kind of all. Its most prevalent symptom is hopelessness.

The counselor asked if I would like to try medication, and I said yes, having heard of no other option. I was going to go to a very reputable psychiatrist, who would give me a prescription for Prozac, and that would be it. I'd be cured.

During our first appointment, the psychiatrist interviewed me and suggested that instead of medication, I should try group therapy. Twice a week, for several hours at a time, I went to a group therapy, where we did relaxation activities and workbook lessons. These methods didn't really work for me either, and I was unsatisfied with the whole experience.

However, at the end of group therapy, I did something completely empowering. I was able to write a note to my psychiatrist telling her everything that was wrong with the class and how I would have done it better. I learned something from this. I realized that while I was depressed and while I was wasting my time in group therapy, time had been passing. I discovered that I wanted the time back, or at least I wanted to stop losing it.

At this point, school was so bad my teachers recommended to my mom that I go to a residential treatment facility (a place where kids go when they don't behave or fit in). I was lucky to have a mother who cared—she wouldn't allow it. Instead, she said, "You're changing schools."

The new school had a policy: there are no bad kids. I ran there, within a matter of days. It was a plain school, uglier than the one I went to before. Inside, however, it was warm and full of life. I had pretty much the same classes, but definitely better teachers. I was still depressed, but I could see clearer now that I was out of the muck from the other school.

At this new school I began making new friends and losing old. This was a good thing. At first, it was impossible for me to say to someone, "I don't like the way you treat me. I won't be your friend." I felt I had to cling to whoever would like me. When I finally did stand up for myself and say this to several people, it was fantastic! I was free!

Another huge step in my recovery process was doing things I enjoyed. I started taking dance lessons again, which I had liked when I was younger. Dance was a helpful release from the depression. I also began putting all of my effort into writing. I would write after school, during class, in the library during lunch, all the time! This eventually paid off because I won a poetry contest, which published a poem of mine in *React Magazine*. Doing things I enjoyed helped me find my true self again and helped pull me out of my depression.

The final accomplishment in my battle with depression was an assembly at school. A woman came and spoke to everyone. Her message was that no matter what you have going on in your life, it's no excuse for not being responsible, not doing things that show you have self-respect. I was fascinated. From that moment on I knew for sure I was okay.

I understand now why so many adults think that hopelessness and apathy are just normal feelings for our generation. Depression seems to be so common with kids our age that it could be called an epidemic. But just because everyone else around you is depressed, that doesn't mean you have to be. The outlook you have inside can make a huge impact on everyone else. It can spread the epidemic or work toward its cure.

While I was depressed I felt totally hopeless and didn't think I'd ever recover. But I'm here to tell you that depression doesn't have to be a problem that you cope with all your life or that kills you. You can get better. My story is here to prove this.

How to Tell If You Are Depressed, or If Someone You Know Is

I don't want my advice to substitute in any way for that of a professional therapist, but I've listed some common symptoms of depression below.

* Sudden changes in behavior, appearance, activities, academics, energy level and mood
* Changes in eating habits
* Constant feelings of hopelessness and even loss of self
* Feeling like everything is permanently wrong
* Feeling constantly tired or unbearably overwhelmed
* Feelings of extreme anxiety and pressure, sometimes to the point of physical illness, like headaches or stomach aches
* Changes in sleeping habits, like having trouble sleeping or sleeping much more than usual
* Any suicidal thoughts, or the feeling that you just want to disappear, must be taken *very* seriously as definite signs of depression.

Sometimes depression shows no clear symptoms at all. That's why it's important to talk about things and to be open. Remember, too, that almost everyone experiences some symptoms of depression at one time or another. But if you or someone you know experiences them the majority of the time, it is a sign that you may be depressed.

If you think you might be depressed, be brave and seek help. Don't let anyone tell you it's shameful to be depressed and don't let anyone promise you an instant solution. If you think a friend might be depressed, talk to her about it. Be direct and tell her that you're worried.

What to Do to Help Yourself or a Friend

Everyone takes their own path out of depression, but it's almost impossible to come out of it without help. You don't have to go through it alone!

Counseling: If you feel you might be depressed, consider talking to your parents about finding a good counselor. Make sure you feel comfortable with the counselor you choose and with the place where you have counseling sessions. Counseling has a lot to do with talking about things you may not otherwise feel safe to say, but you have to be open and honest with your feelings in order for this method to help. And remember that you don't have to stay with a counselor you don't like or don't feel comfortable with. There are plenty more good counselors out there.

Group Therapy: Group therapy is when you meet with a group of people who are experiencing similar things to you. You do exercises or talk together and give each other support. Group therapy can help you identify with other people like you and it can also be a place to share your feelings. Just because it didn't work for me doesn't mean it won't work for you. And like counseling, if you don't feel comfortable with one particular group, try another.

Medication: Many times drugs are used in treating depression, especially when it is severe. Many doctors believe that drugs are an effective way of treating severe depression, but you may have to continue taking them for the rest of your life. Don't be embarrassed if you take medication for depression — it's a medical condition just like any other that might require drug treatment.

A Positive Self-Image: There is another level beyond just coming out of depression. It is gaining a positive image of yourself and allowing yourself the freedom to do what you like. I think anyone can benefit from this, whether they are trying to come out of depression or not. This is especially important for girls, because the way many societies raise us is *not* to have an opinion on things and *not* to do what we enjoy.

The Power List: An easy and helpful exercise to boost your self-image is to create what I call a "Power List." Make a list of all the things that make you feel powerful, no matter how small. They can be anything from voicing your opinion to just being around your friends. Once you have this list, keep it with you. Read it often. How often do you do things listed here? How can you do them more? What new things are you discovering you might want to add? You have my official permission to do whatever you want on that list, as often as you want, no matter what anyone thinks. This is what *you* think. Reawaken your true self, do things to please it and act as wonderful and smart as you really are.

Here are a few things on my Power List. Writing. Working with kids makes me feel powerful because I know I am touching the future. I still like to dance. I like to go hiking. When I'm done I may be tired, but I feel stronger than I did before I started the hike. Being a feminist makes me feel powerful. This means that I speak up about things that wrong me and other women and girls. Not everyone I know feels it's okay for me to do that. They cringe at that word and feel threatened. But others don't—I don't. I don't let people tell me how to think and act, and I have a very strong self-image because of this.

Good Resources

Revolution from Within by Gloria Steinem
A very good overall self-esteem book.

Happiness Is a Choice by Barry N. Kaufman
A refreshing new view on happiness.

Girls Speak Out: Finding Your True Self by Andrea Johnston
Every girl should read this! It deals with issues that are the cause of
depression in many girls.

What You Can Change . . . and What You Can't: The Complete Guide to Self-Improvement by Martin E. P. Seligman, Ph.D.
Gives an understandable definition of depression, explains treatments and
includes an actual depression test.

Learned Optimism by Martin E. P. Seligman, Ph.D.
Teaches you how to be optimistic.

*You Are Not Alone: Words of Experience and Hope for the Journey Through
Depression* by Julia Thorne
Quotes and short stories from people in all stages of depression.

*Dare to Live: A Guide to the Prevention and Understanding of Teenage
Suicide and Depression* by Michael Miller
A guide to teenage depression and suicide.

Some numbers to call if you need to talk to someone

I know it's hard to make these calls, but it's easier than dealing with
the pain alone. Take the first step. Be brave.

Dial 0 and ask for a local crisis and suicide hotline.
Dial 911 and ask for the emergency ward of a local hospital.
Call the **Teenline** at 1-800-522-8336.

How to Save
Your Environment

Sophie Jeannot, age 13

✂ Hobbies: *soccer, volleyball, reading, speech, swimming*

📖 Favorite writer: *Caroline B. Cooney*   📖 Favorite book:

Wait Till Helen Comes   ♬ Hero: *Sandra Bullock*

❀ Dream: *to become a published author or an actress*

My stepdad works at a recycling center, so I'm very interested in ways to save the environment. I live in Seattle, a city which you might not think is polluted, but, like most cities, actually is. One time when I was driving with my dad, I noticed a purplish, greyish cloud of smog. It was forming around the buildings and around major factories. I also realized that there was a lot of paper that was going into dumps when it should be going into recycling centers. This is what finally clued me in. My city is polluted! The next thing I needed to do was figure out how to inform people about the problem which is currently on our hands.

Recycling at Home

Cleaning up the environment may seem like too big a problem, but just start at home and work your way up. If everyone did their small part, the whole world would quickly become a much cleaner place. Recycling is an excellent place to start. Remind your parents to separate trash and returnable bottles. If we didn't recycle, there would be so much trash on the ground you would barely be able to see your own feet!

By recycling paper and paper products, we cut down fewer trees. There is only a limited amount of trees. Sure, you can plant new trees, but you can't replace the destroyed ecosystems. If you cut down one tree it affects the whole forest. Plants and animals that lived on and around that tree die because their habitat is gone; insects and animals that ate those plants and animals also die; and so on. Soon there will be nothing left. Also, all life relies on the forests for oxygen to breathe—people, too! And that's the most important reason why we need to reduce, reuse and recycle.

Conserving Energy

The less resources (like water) and energy (like electricity in your lights) we use, the less resources we need to take from nature, and the less energy we need to produce. Producing energy and taking resources ruins things like rivers (dams and nuclear power plants) and other natural places. Make sure you don't have any leaking faucets or if you do, get them repaired. This is important because if your faucets leak one drop per second, that equals 650 wasted gallons per year! Also turn off all your lights whenever you leave a room to save energy. Both of these not only help save our environment, but also save your family money. You might not have to pay the bills now, but when you get your own house someday you will! It's better to start good habits now while you're young.

Using Earth-Friendly Products

Another way to help is by using products that don't hurt the environment. Buy toiletries from companies that don't test their products on animals. Check the labels for "no animal testing." To help keep the water clean don't buy products which have the words "Toxic", "Danger" or "Warning" on their labels. If they do, they are probably harmful to you and to your environment. Products you use to clean, to take care of your garden, etc. usually have those words on the label. Look for products that are labeled "Earth-Friendly." If you put weed killers on your garden or lawn, the toxins in them will seep down into the earth and eventually get into the water system. This affects everyone's health! The fish and plants in the oceans and rivers will get poisoned by the toxins, as will you. The same thing happens if you pour toxic chemicals down the drain or down a storm drain.

There are many other things you can use, instead of those products, which are much safer. For example, you can use vinegar and water to clean mirrors. Put 1/4 cup (60 ml) of vinegar in a spray bottle and fill the rest with water. Then spray and wipe. For a multi-use cleaner, use liquid Castile soap. There are tons of earth-friendly products and home-made recipes you can use to help save your environment and clean up at the same time! Contact the resources at the end of this chapter for more ideas.

Action In Your Neighborhood

Another thing you can do is have a neighborhood clean-up. To do this you should pass out a flyer to your neighbors with the time and meeting place to begin the clean-up. Example:

NEIGHBORHOOD CLEAN-UP!
NOVEMBER 17th
MEET IN THE CHURCH'S PARKING LOT AT 2:00 P.M.
PICK UP ANY TRASH YOU FIND

You may also want to make it into a party or pot-luck afterward, for the people who helped. If so, mention the party and what time the clean-up will end, in your flyer.

Making A Difference

A very powerful action you can take to save your environment is to write letters to your congressman/woman. Tell them why you want to protect the environment and/or about a particular environmental issue in your area that you are passionate about. You can get their address from your parent, teacher or the library. If your teacher is interested, you could get everyone in your class to write a letter and send them all together. Congressmen/women really pay attention to the letters they receive. They figure that for every letter they receive, at least 10 people out there feel the same way but didn't take the time to write. So your one opinion counts 10 times as much when you write a letter! This is how major changes can get made by individuals like you and me. And it's pretty easy.

Staying  Active

The best thing for you to do is to keep your parents and your friends aware of how important it is to recycle and keep your neighborhood and total environment clean. Remember: everything you do is important, no matter how small you think it is. We only have one world and we have to keep it clean.

If you want to get more information you can call 1-800-RECYCLE. They will send you a whole bunch of things including tattoos, bookmarks, games and flashcards. Remember it's up to you reduce, reuse and recycle.

Other resources to contact for more information and ideas

The Sierra Club
85 2nd St., 2nd floor
San Francisco, CA 94105
(415) 977-5653

Friends Of The Earth
1025 Vermont Ave. NW, 3rd floor
Washington, DC 20005
(202) 783-7400

Treepeople
12601 Mulholand Drive
Beverly Hills, CA 90210
(818) 753-4600

Keep America Beautiful
1010 Washington Blvd.
Stamford, CT 06901
(203) 323-8987

Dealing with Differences

December Kinney, age 10

✂ Hobbies: *writing, reading, jewelry making* ✎ Favorite class: *Social Studies* 📖 Favorite writer: *Frances Hodgson Burnett* ☺ Pet peeve: *dishonest people* 🎵 Hero: *my mom* ❀ Dream: *to become the first African-American, female president of the United States*

I live in a very diverse community and have friends of many different religions and races. Kati is Jewish, Janice is Asian, Erin is Caucasian, Felicia A. is Hispanic, Aneesah is Muslim, Felicia K. is Greek and Kelli and I are African-American. We all get along. I think it's important for girls to know that they can make friends with people who are different from them.

There was a time when I got teased for hanging out with kids who weren't my color or weren't that popular. I've learned how to handle that. I'm also a Peer Mediator at my school—I help kids solve their conflicts and differences. This chapter gives advice on how to make and keep friends who are different from you and what to do if you don't agree on something.

What makes people different?

Natasha: To me, people aren't different. They just have different ideas and beliefs. It's good to be out of the ordinary because nobody knows what the ordinary really is anyway.

Alyssa: People have different tastes in clothes. Also, some people wear glasses, retainers, braces, etc.

Terri: Their personalities, their way of doing things and the way they think.

December: There are lots of things that make people different—different weights, income levels, hobbies, etc. Everyone is unique. Don't be afraid to be the "weird" or "different" one in a group of clones.

What makes you feel different?

Felicia A.: Not a lot of people look like me because where I live there aren't a lot of Mexicans. Also, I dress differently from everyone I know.

Erin: I wear glasses and braces.

Aneesah: My religion. I'm Muslim.

Alyssa: In my school there aren't many kids with one color mother and a different color father.

Victoria: I learn very quickly.

December: I'd probably choose reading a book over watching TV, so I guess you could say I'm a bookworm.

Why are kids mean to people who are different?

Janice: Because they think that the color of their skin makes them inferior to everyone else.

Aneesah: Because they're prejudiced. They may get it from their parents or the people they hang around with.

Kelli: Because they don't have a heart. They just want to gossip and try to impress their friends and boys.

Felicia A.: Because they are afraid or not used to new things. For example, I wear a retainer. At first people said I couldn't talk and they would tease me. But now they're used to it and have learned to accept me as me.

December: Because they make their judgments on what the person looks like on the outside without getting to know the person first. They think, "Oh, this girl's different from me, so she must be bad, weird or lower-class than me."

How do you feel about being in a school with different kinds of kids?

Andrea: I like it because it helps me learn different things. I also dislike it because sometimes they speak different languages in front of me and I feel left out.

Victoria: Good, because you know a variety of people. Also, if there was only one kind of kid in school, when you graduated you wouldn't know how to act around different people.

December: I like it because I know that even though a person may look different from me, I make my judgments based on what a person's like on the inside.

Erin: It feels good as long as they don't make fun of my race or religion. If they do . . . bye!

Felicia K.: I enjoy it because I learn about different cultures, human nature and how people are the same and different. It also makes life more interesting!

How did you get to be friends with people who are different from you?

Alyssa: At my school there are kids of many different backgrounds, so if you have two or more friends, they're most likely to be different from you.

Candis: By talking to people, telling them about myself and learning about them.

Felicia K.: By being open and friendly wherever I went and by participating in different activities.

December: My friends introduce me to different kinds of people.

What if you're afraid to make friends who are different from you?

Natasha: Don't be afraid. Be open. Speak out.

Rebecca: Have your friends introduce you to their friends.

December: Inconspicuously stand near the person, volunteer to do projects with her, pick her for your team in gym, ask her for homework assignments . . . you get the idea!

What if people tease you for making friends with people who are different?

Kelli: If you were an outsider, you would want someone to be nice to you. So would the people who are teasing you. Being different is always difficult. Having someone to talk to and introduce you to people helps.

Melissa: Your real friends won't or shouldn't care or tease you about it.

Erin: Ignore it. It's fun learning about different heritages and stuff that others believe in, as long as you don't betray your own beliefs.

December: It doesn't matter what other people think. If you make friends with someone who's different, soon other people will start being their friend, too.

What should you do if someone teases you about the way you look and/or talk?

Victoria: Tell them they're not very mature.

Janice: Ignore them because it doesn't matter. What matters is what my friends and I think of me.

Felicia A.: Understand that you had no choice how you turned out. Nobody has a choice unless they dye their skin, and I don't want to do that!!! Remember, they're just trying to make you mad.

Melissa: Use your words instead of fighting. Fighting will just get you in trouble and you still won't have solved your problems.

December: Talk about it with someone you know will listen. Also, don't believe what they say, because what you think of yourself affects how other people think of you. If you think badly of yourself, other people will see that and feel the same way about you. But if you feel good about yourself, other people will feel good about you also.

Babysitting Brainstorms

Gitty Braude, age 14

✄ Hobbies: *dancing, writing, sewing, being with my friends and family* ✎ Favorite classes: *Jewish Studies and Math* ♫ Hero: *my mom* ❀ Dream: *that the Messiah will come and bring peace to our world*

I am the oldest girl in my family and have six younger sisters. For the last 14 years, I have been babysitting, playing and helping out with kids. That is the reason why I, out of all people, will really be able to help you out with babysitting ideas. It is very important for babysitters to know how to deal with the kids, not only the money. I will help you babysit kids in ways that will make it fun and interesting for you, too.

Just  for Fun

Here are some fun and original activities to do with the kids.

Carnival

Supplies: Some simple carnival booth supplies. The supplies will depend on which booths you decide to use.

Instructions: You will make a small carnival for the kids. It doesn't have to be anything major, only a small thing you will be able to man on your own. With just two or three booths, it will still be a lot of fun for the kids. Here are several ideas, but again, be creative and come up with your own, too!

• Take a small basket and give about three chances for the children to throw a ball into it.

• Pile empty soda cans on top of each other to form a pyramid shape. Give about three chances to throw a ball and knock them over.

• Fill up a bowl with flour (or sand) and hide pennies inside. The kids will have to search through the flour (or sand) in a given amount of time and try to find the pennies.

* Take a few bowls and fill each one with a different substance. For example, fill one with flour, one with water and one with salt. Blindfold the children and let them feel each substance. See how many they can guess correctly.

Super School

Supplies: Various school supplies.

Instructions: Even though kids don't like school, somehow it becomes a lot of fun when it's played as a game. For desks, I usually use chairs and another chair to sit on. You can just teach simple information, and the kids will enjoy "learning" things they know. This activity can go on for a long time and is loads of fun.

Wrap-Around

Supplies: A small toy or prize that will appeal to the age group you are dealing with, a tape recorder and a music tape.

Instructions: Wrap the prize many times with different layers. For example, wrap it in a piece of paper, then a plastic bag, then gift wrapping, etc. Put the children in a circle and hand the package to one of the kids. When you turn the music on, they will pass the package around. They will keep going until you stop the music, and then the child holding the package will remove one layer. The package continues going around until the prize is uncovered and that child gets to keep it.

Getting Them to Eat

Kids love to eat, right? Right. The only problem is that what they love to eat is usually not food!

Edible Art

Supplies: You may want to get additional foods before coming to the home, but you can probably use whatever food the family has.

Instructions: This method may take a bit of preparation on your part, but it is very worthwhile. You will be taking the regular, boring meal that the child needs to eat and transforming it into something exciting. You will take the food, whatever it may be and cut it or arrange it into a fun picture for the child. Here are a few ideas, but feel free to be creative and make up your own!

- SMILEY FACE: For the eyes, you can use two grapes. Use a small piece of apple for the nose, a slice of orange for the mouth and thin strips of banana as hair.
- GARDEN: For this one, you can use strips of lettuce as grass. Cucumber slices can be stems for flowers, and their blossoms can be round slices of bell pepper. Finish it off with a piece of yellow squash as the sun.
- SNOWMAN: If you're having baked potatoes, carrots and meat for supper, this one will be good for you. First peel the skins off the potatoes. Then mash them up really well. Next, form three balls with the mashed potatoes: a small one, a medium-sized one and a large one. Build your snowman and stick in carrots for the nose and small pieces of meat for the eyes.

Gimme the Junk Food!

Supplies: In addition to the meal the child needs to eat, you will need one type of food or junk food that the child really enjoys.

Instructions: This is for really lousy eaters only. Present the child with the meal. Every time he/she takes a bite, stick a piece of the favorite into a plastic bag. When he or she is all done, the bag with the junk food will be ready to be eaten. This way, the more regular food the child eats, the more junk food he or she will be allowed to eat.

Getting Them to Clean Up

Who really likes to vacuum, wash the dishes or just simply clean up? Certainly not young kids.

Scrub 'n' Sing

Supplies: Yourself, with some brains.

Instructions: Make up a short song or chant to sing as each item gets put away and get the children to sing it with you. Here is an example:

One less thing to go,

We dump the _____ in its bin,

And now the floor may show.

Treasure Hunt

Supplies: A pen and paper.

Instructions: If you have a big mess, this one will work for you. On small pieces of paper, write different consequences for the kids. Write things like, "Do ten jumping jacks, skip around the room and stand on your head for a minute." (The consequences will depend on the age group you are dealing with.) Then take the papers and hide them among the mess. For example, you could put them underneath toys on the floor. When a child comes across one of the papers, everyone will stop and watch as he or she follows its instructions. After a few items are cleaned up, add a couple more consequence papers. Do this until everything is clean.

Clean-up Tag

Supplies: A pen and paper.

Instructions: This solution is for two or more children. Give each child a piece of paper which says all the things they need to clean up or put away. Count to three, and then have them all start the jobs. When each job is done, the child will come and touch your hand and run back to do the next thing on the list, until the entire list is done. The winner gets a prize, like getting the first bedtime story, picking the movie, etc.

Getting Them to Go to Bed

Any babysitter knows that no young child (or even older one) enjoys going to bed. As soon as bedtime arrives, the house is too scary, the sheets are too scratchy and a thousand more things need to be done.

Sleeping Beauty Race

Supplies: Only you.

Instructions: Tell the kids that whoever gets ready for bed will be able to play a fun game. When they are all ready, have the children stand at the doorway of the bedroom. Explain to them that at the count of three, everyone has to run to their beds and lie very still, making no sounds. Every time they move around or make noise, they will get one "out." Whoever gets the least "outs" will be the winner and will be informed by the parents in the morning. Eventually they should fall asleep, but don't forget to tell their parents who won, or else the next time they won't believe that it's a real game. If there is only one child, she will be testing herself to see how few outs she can get.

Goodnight Game

Supplies: An exciting new game—maybe a board game from your own home.

Instructions: This is a good one to do awhile before bedtime. Don't show the kids the game you brought, but invite them all to play. The conditions you will tell them are: 1) Everyone must be ready for bed before the game starts; 2) When the time comes for the game to be put away, there will be no arguing. When you tell them this, it makes them take more responsibility for their actions. Before you start, make sure they understand all the conditions fully and agree to comply. They will most probably be curious to see what you have and readily agree. Have fun!

Bus Stop

Supplies: Only you.

Instructions: Line up all of the kids behind you as if you are the bus driver and they are the passengers. Pretend you are driving the bus, and with all the kids following behind you, take the first child to the room where he or she needs to do something in order to get ready for bed. The kids are not allowed to leave the room until you come and pick them up with the bus. Continue on your rounds, picking up and dropping off all the kids where they belong. While in the rooms, the children will have to get their pajamas, brush their teeth and do anything else they need to do before going to bed. Before you know it, they will all be ready for bed. Note: This can also be adapted for getting dressed or any other chore.

An Extra Tip

When their parents are leaving, many times children cry, and it is hard to calm them down. The simplest solution is to distract the children. Instead of trying to tell them that their parents will come home soon, start talking to them about something else, making jokes or tickling them. You can also get them involved in a fun game or activity.

And Don't Forget . . .

1. Make sure to find out where the parents will be and have the phone number there in case of an emergency.

2. Always have fire and police department numbers handy.

3. Be sure you know what to do in case of an earthquake, tornado, hurricane or any other natural disaster, depending on where you live.

4. Before the parents leave, find out what the children's bedtimes are.

5. Most importantly, don't forget to bring your patience and your smile to the kids!

What to Do About Drugs

Tarrin Petersen, age 12

✂ Hobbies: *swimming, reading, writing, art class* ✎ Favorite class: *Science* 📖 Favorite book: The Ballad of Lucy Whipple ☺ Pet peeve: *people who are racist* ♫ Heroes: *Jane Goodall and Summer Sanders* ❀ Dream: *to go to the Olympics*

Jane Schwarz, age 13

✂ Hobbies: *acting, singing, dancing, horseback riding, basketball, surfing the Net, football, baseball* ✎ Favorite classes: *Math, Leadership* 📖 Favorite writer: *Stephen King* ♫ Hero: *my mom, Celia Schwarz* ❀ Dreams: *to go to Harvard, get my Ph.D. and become a pediatrician*

Most of you reading this chapter should know what a drug is. You might think of crack, cocaine, pot, etc. But these are not the only kinds of drugs. There are lots more common addictive substances we see every day, such as cigarettes, alcohol and caffeine. Abusing harmful substances can ruin relationships, families and friendships. That's why this information can be extremely helpful.

Why We Don't Do Drugs

Tarrin: I don't do drugs because I know what smoking alone has done to my grandmother. She almost died because of cigarettes. Another reason that I don't do drugs is because I'm an athlete, and if I did drugs, they would alter my athletic performance. Besides that, I don't want to go to prison!

Jane: The main reason I don't do drugs is because I know the dangerous effects they can have on your body and mind, and I don't want that to happen to me. I know several people who have done drugs on an experimental basis, and I've seen what it has done to them. Their mental state has declined, their physical health is not what it used to be and their grades have dropped drastically. I want to go to Harvard, and it would be pretty hard to get in if I'm getting C's and D's in school.

Q: I've been invited to a party where I think there might be drugs or alcohol. All the "cool people" will be there and I want to go, too, but I don't want to do drugs. How can I say "no" without looking like a goody-goody?

A: This is a very tough situation that many of us face throughout adolescence. There are several methods for solving this problem. The first and most simple technique is to simply "Just say no," like all those cheesy commercials suggest. Chances are that the person asking you won't persist if you say no the first time. Probably the only reason they would keep asking was if you showed any hesitation or thought it over for too long.

Another method would be to lie and tell the user that you're allergic to the substance being offered. If you think about it, this is actually not much of a lie. To be allergic to something means your body reacts to it in an unwanted way when you ingest it. Your body reacts this way when you're drunk or high.

If the peer pressure persists, we suggest you just leave. You're better off not arguing with people who might be high, as they tend to act irrationally. It would be safer to go home.

Q: My friend confided in me that she has used illegal drugs. I am very worried about her, but I don't want to lose her trust by telling anyone. What should I do?

A: If your friend tells you something like this or if you suspect she is doing drugs, but she hasn't admitted it yet, the most critical thing to do is to find out what sort of habit she has. It may not be as serious as you think. If it was just a one-time thing or an experiment, you should probably just forget it. Find out if she intends to do it again any time soon.

If it seems like it's happened a lot, there are many things you can do to help her. There's hope for your friend. You could confide in a school counselor or another trusted adult, using a fake name for your friend, of course. Ask them for hotline numbers or places you could write or call for professional information.

Another possible solution would be to subtly tell your friend that you have noticed a change in her behavior and you've been wondering what's going on lately. If she blows up at you, tell her it was just an innocent question coming from a concerned friend. You have a right to be concerned about her health.

Although it may seem stupid, probably the best thing you can do for your friend is to show her how much fun you're having without drugs. Show her other ways to feel good without smoking a joint. Go to parties (sober), prank call crushes, go shopping, eat junk food, dance, bike, ski, swim . . . the possibilities for drug-free fun are endless! It's up to you to remind her of this.

As painful as it seems, there is only so much you can do to help your friend. If you have tried all these other options, it is really up to her whether she will choose to ruin her life over this or not. If worse comes to worst, there are community health programs run by drug counselors in most areas. You could go to one of their meetings and get some advice. If it really gets serious, make sure you've informed her parents and then maybe set up a visit with a counselor with all of you. You could disguise the plan as a trip to the mall in order to convince her to go. This last  option will definitely threaten your friendship, but that may be what it takes.

Q: At school we're always told "smokers are bad people." My mother smokes and I worry about her health, but I don't think she's a bad person. What should I do?

A: You're right. Your mother isn't a bad person. She has an addiction. Of course, it would be best if she quit, but you probably can't make her do it.

She's a grown-up and she makes her own choices. What you can do is this:

Read up on the health problems associated with smoking. Become totally informed and then tell your mother your concerns. Tell her what you've learned about what she's doing to her body and why you're worried about her. If you don't nag at her, but just tell her how much you love her and want her to be healthy, she'll probably listen. You might try telling her about the different ways to quit and offer to help her. But be prepared that she may not quit just to make you feel better. For someone who has never smoked, it is virtually impossible to grasp how hard it is to give up. Most people who try to quit don't succeed on their first try. But if they *keep* trying, then eventually they can beat it. Each time they try to quit it gets easier and easier.

Q: People in my family are doing drugs and I don't want to be involved! I also don't want to see my family in trouble with their health or the law! What should I do?

A: Even if everyone in your family drinks or does drugs, there is no reason you have to do them, too. There are many patterns to drug use and reasons why you shouldn't continue them.

First of all, your family's patterns may have started when people were uneducated about the results of drug use. That person who began using drugs may be an older member of your family like a grandparent, aunt or uncle or maybe even a parent. Maybe everyone around them responded positively to certain drugs, so they thought it was okay for them to use, too. The cause of all this is obvious: lack of education. No one really knew about all the problems that arise from drug use until recently. Many people have been addicted for a very long time. Since doctors have discovered all the diseases and illnesses that result from drug use, we now know a lot more than we did 20 years ago. This is the opportunity for you to help a different generation get healthy.

Before we tell you how, ask yourself these questions:

• How many people in your family smoke or drink?

- How many do illegal drugs?
- Have any family members died from drugs or alcohol?
- Have any family members talked to you about drug use?
- Have any family members pressured you into doing any form of drugs? Did you try it?
- Have any of these family members quit abusing drugs or alcohol?

Think about your answers. How do they reflect on your family? Do you need outside advice? If you do, perhaps the rest of this chapter will help. Remember that if someone in your family offers you drugs or responds to you violently because of them, that is a crime and that person is in huge trouble. If that ever happens, you should call a hotline, or talk to teachers, safe family members or even the police. Don't be afraid to protect yourself even though it's family. No matter who they are, no one should ever harm you.

Q: Recently I began experimenting with drugs and now I think I'm hooked! I've found ways to hide it from my parents, but I feel horrible and totally regret trying it at all. What can I do?

A: The saying "curiosity killed the cat" doesn't have to apply to you. Ask yourself why you started experimenting in the first place. Were your "friends" experimenting? Did they tease you for not trying it? Were you trying to be like everyone else?

The first step to quitting is admitting you have a problem and deciding you don't want to do it any more. You've already done that, so you're well on your way. The next step is to get help and more information. In most towns there are community health organizations that specialize in drug rehabilitation. They can give you tons of information, answer your questions and help you get over your addiction in confidentiality at a low price or no cost at all.

If a drug counselor is too scary or impersonal for you, find someone you can trust and ask for help. Our first suggestion is to tell your parents or guardian the truth. You will feel better and they will be glad you told before it was too late. They may be upset, but they'd be a lot more upset if you got in trouble later. But if your parents/guardian aren't available or are unapproachable for some reason, here are some other ideas: teachers, school counselors, a friend's parents, aunt, uncle, cousin or other older siblings.

People will most likely not be angry with you for confessing your problem, but will instead admire your strength and bravery for doing something about it.

Here are some other things you can do on your own to quit: make a mental note of how, where and who you get drugs from. Avoiding those places and people will help you quit. An easy and healthy way to help quit is to find a hobby or sport to keep you occupied. Obviously, if you are spending your day getting high, you have a little too much time on your hands. Working out at a neighborhood gym or joining a swim team will keep you busy and fit and make you feel really good about yourself. Besides sports, the arts are a great way to release your feelings. Learn how to paint, do pottery or write. These activities will make you feel stronger and better about yourself and will help you find the strength to quit. But quitting alone is very hard—we recommend you do these things *and* ask someone for help.

Q: I recently found out that the boy I've been dating does drugs. I don't want to do them, but I really like him. I'm afraid if he offers me some and I say no, he'll dump me. What should I do?

A: Right now you are in a sticky situation. You can either continue to date him and risk being offered drugs or you can stop dating him and risk a broken heart. Let's review your options.

Suppose you continue to date him and he does offer you drugs. There is a slight chance you could end up doing drugs whether you want to or not. That's peer pressure. Do you like him so much you would do anything for him? That's a dangerous kind of relationship to be in.

If you stopped dating him, you wouldn't have to say no to drugs or feel pressured to do anything. If you break up with him, remember that there are plenty of great guys out there who don't spend their time on an artificial high.

If you choose to continue dating him, tell him how you feel. Tell him you don't want to be involved with drugs and it hurts you to see him ruining himself with this substance. He may ignore you or dump you. At this point, you have to ask yourself if the relationship is really worth the trouble. For further advice, follow what we suggested for a best friend's problem.

Q: Many people at my school do drugs. I think it would be a safer and more appealing place if the druggies were more informed about the dangers. What can I do to change it around here?

A: First of all, it's superb that you want to help educate people on this. There are endless activities you can start. Before you start anything, talk to a teacher or a member of the staff about your concerns. They may have some ideas, too.

One effective way to spread the word is to hold a poster contest. Each poster would have an anti-drug message or information. Choose several winners and make color copies of the posters so they can be hung all around the school.

If you have time to make some phone calls, create a sobriety club and locate a public speaker who overcame a substance addiction and would feel comfortable talking to a group of kids about it.

Running for an office in school leadership would also help you spread your word. Other students and friends would be very likely to listen to your ideas. I'm sure there are a lot more ideas that will show that drugs and alcohol are not what they're cracked up to be. Good luck!

Sprinkler Fun

Devon Amelia diLauro, age 12

✂ Hobbies: *singing in the Singing Angels, drawing, skating, writing, swimming, tap dancing* 📖 Favorite writer: *Nancy Levene* ⊗ Pet peeve: *when kids brag or show off* ☠ Hero: *Mrs. Broadbent, my third grade teacher, who got me interested in writing* ❀ Dream: *to become an artist or choreographer*

In the summer I am always trying to think of fun activities to do. One thing I often do if I am bored is make up booklets, stories or plays and illustrate them. "Sprinkler Fun" is a book of water games I wrote to help children cool off on hot days.

For each activity, girls should wear bathing suits and have a towel to dry off with. Make sure that the water pressure isn't hard enough to hurt anyone. A garden hose nozzle could be used to adjust the amount of spray.

Water  Limbo

No. of Players: 3 or more
Equipment: garden hose

Have one person hold a hose and let everyone else limbo under it. Lower the stream of water after everyone has had a turn going under it at the same level. If someone touches the stream of water, they are out. The last player to get wet is the winner.

The Serpent  Sees

No. of Players: 3 or more
Equipment: blindfold, garden hose

Before you start playing this game, decide on boundary areas to which players may run. Pretend that the hose is a snake. Blindfold one player.

That person holds the hose and moves the stream of water all around. Everybody tries to dodge the water. The first player to get wet is the next blindfolded person.

Make the  Grade

No. of Players: 3 or more
Equipment: garden hose

One person holds a garden hose a few inches (centimeters) above the ground. That person says "Preschool." Everyone else tries to jump over the stream of water without getting wet. Raise the garden hose a couple of inches (cm) for each grade level. Go all the way to 12th grade—Preschool, Kindergarten, 1st grade, 2nd, 3rd, 4th, 5th, 6th, 7th, 8th, Freshman (9th), Sophomore (10th), Junior (11th), Senior (12th). The first person to get wet holds the hose and starts over with Preschool.

High-Low

No. of Players: 3 or more
Equipment: garden hose

Have one player hold the garden hose and move it up and down. Start by holding the hose high, count to five slowly, then lower the hose, keeping it low for a five count. As the game goes on, move the stream of water faster to make the game more challenging. The other players should try to run under the water when the stream is up high and over it when it is low. If a person touches the stream of water, they are out. The last one to touch is the winner.

Slick  Slide

No. of Players: 2 or more
Equipment: garden hose or sprinkler, long plastic sheet

Set up the sprinkler to spray on the sheet of plastic. The other players should run up to the sheet and slide on their stomachs. Keep the surface wet to make the plastic slick. If you are using a garden hose, take turns being the one to spray the plastic.

* Be careful of rocks and sticks, especially at the landing! Don't forget to dry out the plastic sheet before putting it away.

Swingin'  Sprinkler

No. of Players: 1 or more

Equipment: sprinkler, swing or slide

Set up the sprinkler in front of the swing and then swing back and forth into the spray. If you have a slide, you can slide into the spray.

Have  a Ball!

No. of Players: 3 or more

Equipment: garden hose with spray attachment, beach ball

One player aims the garden hose toward the players, who are trying to play catch with the ball. Move the hose back and forth so that the spray makes it more difficult to throw and catch the ball. The person holding the hose may stop the water anytime, and the player holding the ball when the water stops has to hold the hose for the next game.

Our Bodies, Health & Looks

Raquel "Rocky" Martinez, age 13

✄ Hobbies: *writing, listening to music, drawing, painting, skating, doing aerobics* ✎ Favorite class: *Science* ☺ Pet peeve: *when people lie* ♫ Hero: *my mom* ❀ Dream: *to be a flight attendant and travel the world*

I am writing about body, health and looks because I want girls my age to look and feel good about themselves. There is so much information that girls need to know but don't. I hope my chapter will help you know almost everything you need or want to know about your body, health and looks.

This chapter will include stuff to help you while you are on your period, good exercising tips, how to eat right, make-up tips, most commonly asked questions from teen girls and lots more interesting stuff. I am sure you will enjoy reading this chapter on body, health and looks and learn a lot, too.

Your  Body

Your body is a very important part of life. There are many functions of your body that are happening, have happened or are soon to happen. For those who have grown up already, you are probably wondering if what has happened is normal. For those who are going through these sudden changes, you may be wondering if your body is working right or if there is something wrong with you. And for those of you who have no idea what is going to happen, so that you won't be in sudden shock when it does happen, I will tell you what should happen, what is happening or what will happen. So here it goes.

Growing Hair

Hair will probably start growing practically everywhere. On legs, armpits, privates and even some facial hair. BUT DON'T PANIC. If you hate the facial hair so much that you just can't stand it, go see a doctor. Do not shave your face or put hair removal cream on it unless your doctor recommends it because the hair could grow back darker. For your legs and armpits, go ahead and shave them. You will probably start getting this hair between 9 and 14 years of age.

Getting Breasts

Between the ages of 9 and 15 you will start getting breasts. When they start to develop they will hurt like they have bruises on them; they really don't, they just feel like they do. Sometimes they could hurt really bad and other times they will hurt just a little. You may notice they are all of a sudden uneven. Don't freak yourself out about this because, believe it or not, they will even out in the end.

Other girls may start wearing bras before you. Don't despair! What I would do is go out and buy a bra, even if you don't need one. It will make you feel more normal and like you belong. And no one has to know.

Your Period

Between the ages of 8 and 19 you'll experience another change—your period. The average age that girls start is 12 1/2. This will probably be one of the biggest changes for you. Not to scare you, but this may be one change you will hate. But it is something every girl has to deal with. It's just a fact of life. You will get this once a month. But when you first start, everything in your body will be trying to adjust to your changes, so everything at first won't be on a schedule—it might take a little while.

When you do get on a schedule or you think you have, mark on your calendar when you start, when you should stop and when you should start again, so you won't be surprised. Some girls have cycles as long as 50 days or as short as 20 days, but the average is about 28 days. Count 28 days from when you started to when you should start again. This gives a pretty accurate guess of when you should start.

I remember the first time I started my period. It was when I was 11 during the summer. I went into the bathroom because I felt kind of constipated, and when I got in there I saw some brown clumpy stuff on my underwear. I yelled for my mom to come in and check it out. I had a feeling what it was, but wasn't sure exactly what to do. She showed me what to do and then it was over.

I had a friend once who had started, but nobody ever told her what was going to happen, so when it did happen she thought she was going to die. Of course she didn't, and I told her what was happening to her. She's doing fine now and knows all about it.

Your friends may get their periods before you or vice-versa. This can be uncomfortable if they're all talking about it. If you're embarrassed about it, just don't tell anyone you haven't started yet (or that you have). No one will know if you don't tell them.

Deciding when and if to use tampons is up to you. If you decide you want to use tampons, begin probably two years after you start your period. That will give you a chance to get used to having your period first.

If you choose to use tampons, you need to know about Toxic Shock Syndrome (TSS). TSS is a rare but serious disease that you can die from. Some cases are believed to be caused by tampons, but men and children can get it, too. The symptoms of TSS are: sudden fever, vomiting, diarrhea, fainting or near fainting, dizziness and/or a sudden rash that looks like a sunburn. If any of these symptoms appear, remove your tampon and see a doctor IMMEDIATELY. To avoid getting tampon-related TSS, it is recommended that you use low-absorbency tampons (smaller ones instead of the Super Plus kind) and change your tampon as often as the pack says to. You might also consider using pads at night and tampons only during the day.

Taking the Shape of a Woman

This is a very good change. You are finally growing up and people might just start treating you like you are older than three. Many girls, however, have a hard time dealing with these changes. Even me. One day at school I heard these guys talking about me, so I continued to listen to what they were saying. I found out they were talking about the size of my breasts. They were laughing and saying, "Man did you see her chest? It's as flat as mine." They were saying that kind of stuff about a lot of girls in

school and a lot of the stuff they were saying wasn't even true. But hearing them say that hurt my feelings.

I learned a trick and soon forgot about the whole thing. If someone ever says something like that to you, just think of a time when somebody said something good to you or about you, then give the person who said the bad thing a look that tells him he's dumb. It works almost every time.

Nobody's perfect. Everyone has flaws. I don't like my big forehead or wearing glasses. If everyone was perfect the world would be a very boring place because everyone would look like a model. But to tell you a secret, models don't really look that good. Everyone wishes they could look like the beautiful women you see in the magazines. Skinny, big breasts, perfect hair, perfect face, perfect body. Just perfect, right? WRONG!

These women are so fake. Most of them don't really have big breasts; they just have implants. They use a special thing that they put on themselves to make them have a flat tummy. Then they get in their dress or whatever they are going to wear and they pin it up and the photographer starts taking pictures. Then after all of that, they take the picture and put it into a computer. If anything is wrong with the picture, they change it. If they don't like the colors, they change them. If one strand of hair is out of place, they fix it. If her eyelashes are too short, they make them longer. They can change anything they want to on the computer.

So now has your perspective changed? I know mine did when I first heard that. Each of us has at least one thing we don't like about ourself, even if it's the tiniest thing. But just remember and remind yourself that it's okay, because that's one of the things that makes you, YOU!

Body Odor

Now for the part you all have been waiting for: the section on body odor. Ohhhhhh!! Body odor is something everybody has. Hopefully the person you sit next to in class doesn't have it too bad. If you have bad body odor and do not know how to get rid of it, read up on all four types of body odor, including bad breath.

134

Your Stinky Stinky Armpits: If your armpits stink even when you use deodorant, try using a deodorant soap when taking a bath or shower. This will kill more bacteria than a regular soap. If you are using a spray deodorant, try switching to a stick or roll-on, because they get onto the surface of your pits and work better. I can't tell you the best deodorant because everyone is different, and one that may work for me may not work for you. So try different ones and see which works best for you.

Private Parts: Make sure you clean yourself with a bacterial soap and wear clean underwear. Cotton underwear are the most preferred for ventilation.

Feet that Reek: If you have really stinky feet, use the same soap you use for your armpits. Dry your feet well after you take a shower or bath, especially if you plan on wearing socks. Wet feet under socks can lead to very stinky feet. And I don't think you want that. You can use a deodorant spray if it gets really bad, or if that doesn't seem to work, go see a doctor.

Horrible Bad Breath: To get rid of bad breath, use mouth wash, brush after every meal if possible and brush your tongue! This thing about brushing your tongue may sound funny, but it really does work. Gum also seems to help me.

Your  Health

There is healthy and unhealthy. You may think you are healthy, but you may not be. Or you may think that you are unhealthy when in reality you are actually healthy. I know it sounds kind of confusing, but it's true. So read on to see if you are healthy or unhealthy, how to eat right and how much exercise is right for you.

Food

Here is a food chart that tells you what the food groups are and how much you should eat per day of each group.

FOOD GROUP	BODY-BUILDING FOODS	SERVINGS PER DAY
Milk and milk products		2-4
Protein foods		2-3
Fruits and vegetables		2-3
Breads and cereals		6-11

You should eat at least two to four servings of milk or milk products like yogurt, cottage cheese, ice cream and cheese. Protein foods include eggs, nuts, fish, beans, seeds and meats. Eat at least two to three fruits and vegetables. More if possible. Breads and cereals include things like noodles, biscuits, taco shells, tortillas and popcorn. And of course, try not to eat too much junk food. If your parents serve you unhealthy meals, ask them to get healthier stuff for you or ask if you can make your own meals.

And finally, don't go overboard all of the time when you eat. It's okay once in a while, like when you're really hungry or on the holidays, but don't overdo it all of the time. And never stop eating—that's the worst thing you could ever do.

Anorexia and Bulimia

There are two major eating disorders: anorexia and bulimia. These eating disorders affect many girls our age, are very dangerous, lead to tons of health problems and can even cause death. Generally, girls who are perfectionists and have low self-esteem are more likely to get these disorders. Controlling their food is how they feel in control of their life.

Bulimia is when you eat a ton (binge) and then throw it up (purge). This is what I call just plain gross. I had two friends who had this problem and they didn't look like they were getting any skinnier. A few of the symptoms of bulimia are yellow teeth and bad breath, and it can be deadly.

Anorexia is when you just stop eating or exercise compulsively because you think you're fat. It is a very horrible disease that makes the person think they are fat when they really aren't. Their whole lives become centered around food and weight. There are so many girls who have this problem. Most of them have other problems in their lives, too. Whether it's at home, at school or a problem only they know about, their anorexia usually starts when someone tells them that they need to lose some weight or tells them right out they are fat. This is a very serious problem and anyone can have it. I had two friends who had anorexia.

It's not very fun having friends with eating disorders, so I'm sure it's completely awful to have one yourself. If you or one of your friends have one of these disorders, get help fast, whether it's for them or you. Signs to watch for if you suspect your friend has an eating disorder are: skipping meals, lying about what they eat, major weight loss or gain, obsessive exercising, and/or going to the bathroom directly after each meal.

These disorders are just not worth it. They can really mess up your body and your mind—we're talking about loss of periods, fainting and dizziness, heart, kidney and stomach damage, panic attacks, growing extra body hair, tooth decay, bowel damage, depression and insomnia. Not fun. Anorexia and bulimia don't help you lose weight in the long run — they give you more problems than you already have and they can even kill you.

Exercise

Exercising is very important to being healthy, but you must also eat and drink lots of water. It takes 20 minutes to get your heart working at a good rate, so you should exercise for at least that long. If you don't, the 10-15 minutes that you exercised wasn't worth it because it didn't help anything. If you are a beginner, you should work out for about 20-30 minutes two or three times a week. If you are in moderate shape, work out for 25-35 minutes three to four times a week. For someone in excellent shape, you can work out for 30-45 minutes four to five times a week.

There are countless exercises that you can do in a 20 minute period. Here are my three faves: 1) Jog or power walk. 2) Crunches are a very good abdominal workout that really help flatten the tummy. 3) Push ups and pull ups really help to get you buff—but not as buff as the women you see in the muscle magazines, just enough so you have a little bit of curve in your arm.

Now, exercising is part of looks, but also part of health. You must stay healthy to look good; you must eat right and exercise. You should start to see the results of your workouts in about four weeks. But in order to see results, you need to have a regular exercise routine and healthy eating habits. You *don't* need to starve yourself to get in better shape.

Your  Looks

Make-Up

If you don't feel like wearing make-up, then don't. Lots of girls and women choose never to wear it and look fantastic without it. You really shouldn't do it just because everyone else does. Only do it if you think you're ready and you think you'd look better with it on. If you choose to wear make-up, you should know the right colors for your skin and not put too much on. Here's a chart to see what colors are right for you:

SKIN COLOR	EYES	CHEEKS	LIPS
Fair	pale pinks or light bronze	dusty rose	light mocha, soft mauve or pink
Golden	light browns or gold	bronze	milk shake or any natural shade
African-American	dark berry or deep brown	burgundy	raisin or mahogany
Olive	deep brown or mauve	wine or plum	light mocha or cranberry
Asian	shimmery bronze or spice	sienna	light mocha or toffee
Freckled	peach or warm brown	coral	warm beige or soft brown

Now that you know the best colors of make-up to use for your skin color, try them and see how they look. If these colors don't work, then try something else close to that color.

Skin Care

Pimples, whiteheads, blackheads and other lumps, bumps and blotches on your face — 'most everyone gets these at one point or another. So don't feel like you're the only one who gets a disgusting, blotchy, pimpled-up face. To fight bad skin, wash your face every night before you go to bed and every morning when you wake up. If you do, you may start to see a difference. Different soaps work for different people, so you may have to try a few before you find one you like. I use non-allergenic soap and face lotions, and they work really well for me. If washing doesn't help, try some anti-acne creams from the store. And if that doesn't work, you should see a doctor. They have medicines that are very strong.

Conclusion

Now that you have read my chapter on body, health and looks, I hope you can go away believing that you can look good. You can feel good about yourself because you are special just the way you are, the way God made you! You must remember, you are not the only one who has ever had a big forehead or a crooked toe or whatever it is that you just hate about yourself. I have another tip: look for people with the same flaws as you. It is always reassuring when you see other people with the same flaws. Also, remember not to point out anybody else's imperfections; I am positive they already know! I hope you had a fun time reading my chapter and I hope you learned a lot!

Make a Difference — Volunteer

Amanda Edgar, age 10

✂ Hobbies: *dancing, drawing, figure skating, collecting dolls, shells and gemstones* 📖 Favorite writer: *Shel Silverstein*
☹ Pet peeve: *when my mother says, "Clean your room!"*
♬ Hero: *Rebecca Little, my second grade teacher, who taught our class about volunteering. She is warm and caring—I'd like to be like her.* ❀ Dreams: *to be an elementary school teacher, to teach dance and continue dancing on stage*

I started volunteering when I was four. There was an old man in a wheelchair who came to my church with neighbors because he had no family. One day I noticed that no one was talking to him, so I walked up and started chatting. My mother and I started visiting him at his home. My mom made soups for him and I made pictures and picked him flowers. When he was moved from his home to a nursing home, we still visited him. I think we brightened his life because we gave him attention and were kind to him. We visited him until he died. I felt wonderful because I knew I was helping a person who needed help and special care.

Many people become involved as volunteers because they want to make a difference in the world. Volunteering isn't just for adults; kids can get involved, too!

Volunteering at Home

Help Out: You don't even have to leave your own home to be a volunteer. When I am at home, I help out by dusting and by playing with my younger brother. Doing these things makes me feel good about myself because I am helping my family. Look around your own home and do something you are not expected to do.

Grow a Garden: Another thing my family does to assist others is to plant a garden. We share the extra produce with our neighbors. We have also donated some vegetables to a shelter. My mother makes jams and relishes, and she donates the canned goods to fairs at our church and to a local children's home to help them raise money.

Save Those Soup Can Labels: Before recycling, we always remove the Campbell's Soup™ labels and mail them to St. Jude's Ranch for Children at P.O. Box 60100, Boulder City, NV 89006. Their phone number is 1-800-492-3562. St. Jude's Ranch receives labels from people all across the United States and they use the labels to purchase vans, computers and other things which help the abused children they take care of. Many other organizations collect Campbell's Soup labels. So save your labels and find your favorite organization which collects them. It's an easy way to help.

Donate Clothes/Toys: Instead of throwing out clothes that you've outgrown, find a worthwhile charity for them. My brother and I send some of our outgrown clothing to the children of a missionary couple. We also donate old clothing, toys and household items to the Military Order of the Purple Heart, an organization which aids disabled veterans. (The Purple Heart operates in Pennsylvania, New Jersey, Ohio, Michigan and Texas, so look in your phone book for similar organizations.) The Salvation Army is another organization that needs these kinds of donations. You may decide to sort through your old toys, have a garage sale and donate the money you raise to your favorite charity.

Raise Seeing Eye Dogs: You may decide to volunteer as a family for a special organization. My neighbors, the Wagners, raised approximately 17 Seeing Eye puppies over a period of ten years. The Wagner children helped with this project, and the kids learned a lot about themselves and had a good time with the puppies. Giving the dogs back to The Seeing Eye organization was very hard emotionally, but they knew that each dog would have a very special role in the life of a blind person. Once the Wagners finished training a puppy, they would start the process all over again. The Seeing Eye places puppies in homes in New Jersey, Delaware, Maryland, some counties of Pennsylvania and one county in New York. If you are interested in raising Seeing Eye dogs, contact The Seeing Eye, P.O. Box 375, Morristown, NJ 07963-0375; phone: (201) 539-4425.

Guide Dogs for the Blind places puppies in California, Utah, Oregon, Arizona, Washington, Colorado and Nevada. Contact them at P.O. Box 151200, San Rafael, CA 94915; phone: 1-800-295-4050.

Local Involvement

Collect Food: Something you could do to help in your community is to collect canned goods for a food bank. Various organizations have food available for people in need. Some churches have food pantries, and homeless shelters, women's shelters, etc. could all use canned goods donations. Each year the Boy Scouts have a food drive, so you could contact your local Boy Scout troop (look in the phone book for your area office) to make a donation. Or you can call agencies in your area to see if they need donations. You could even collect food from your friends and neighbors to make a bigger donation. Some organizations, such as our local Red Cross shelter, need donations of diapers, school supplies and holiday gifts for the people who live at the shelter.

Be a Secret Pal: You can help around the neighborhood by being a "secret pal" to a sick or handicapped child. Mail or drop off little gifts, like books or something special that you make. Help an older neighbor with snow shoveling or yard work. Your neighbors would love it if you would volunteer to help them. If you know somebody who is ill, you could make soup or dinner for them. Even sending just a card or picking someone flowers shows them that you care.

Help at School: Volunteering at school would be doing things like helping to shelve library books. I help a first-grade child with reading and so can you! If you see trash on the ground, pick it up, as it will help the janitor.

Be a help around your school.

Adopt a Grandparent: Volunteering at a nursing home will be beneficial for anyone. It will cheer up the patient who may not have many visitors, and you will feel good about yourself, too. I have gone into the nursing home during the holiday times to sing with my Girl Scout troop and also with my second grade class. I also helped other children at my church recently make flower pots with spring bulbs to put in the rooms of some nursing home patients. You may be able to find a patient who does not have any family nearby and "adopt" them to visit. If it would be hard for you to visit, you may be able to mail them cards and letters to cheer them up. Homemade gifts you give to your "adopted grandparent" would always be cherished.

Pet Therapy: My neighbor, Mrs. Wagner, is involved with Pet Therapy. She takes her very friendly cat and dog into nursing homes. The cat is very affectionate and will sit in the laps of many patients. In some cases, the people will respond to the animals when they wouldn't respond to anything else. If you want to be involved in animal-assisted activities or pet therapy opportunities, contact The Delta Society at 289 Perimeter Rd. East, Renton, WA 98055-1329; phone: (206) 226-7357. The Delta Society will be able to tell you about opportunities in your home state.

If you decide to volunteer in the community, you may find out that you have to be a certain age and have working papers. Working papers are required by child labor laws even for some volunteer positions. Many organizations, such as hospitals, may require that you be 14 with working papers; however, you could volunteer there without working papers if your parent volunteers with you.

Explore Your Interests

Nature Lovers: You may want to volunteer at a place where you have an interest. If you are worried about the environment, you may wish to help at a nature center. There are many things to do, such as feeding the birds and animals, working on the grounds, straightening books in the library, stuffing envelopes and helping the staff in other areas.

Book Lovers: If you like books, consider helping in the local library. You could help shelve books, label new books and read to younger children.

Animal Lovers: The Society for the Prevention of Cruelty to Animals (S.P.C.A.) has a need for people to walk dogs, groom the animals, clean cages, feed the animals, clerical help, etc. My parents used to volunteer at the S.P.C.A. as dog walkers and groomers. There are so many places, such as zoos, or animal shelters, etc. which could use your help.

Use Your Talents

You could use your talents when volunteering. A talented teenager named Amy O'Connor is going to major in musical theater at college. She volunteers at our church by directing the youth in musicals. The Red Cross shelter in my area welcomes kids with special talents such as magic acts, singing, etc. to come and share them with the children in the shelter.

Volunteering could lead to career opportunities. My former babysitter, Monica Ardelean, volunteered at a nursery when she was 11. When Monica was older, she also volunteered at our local hospital. Monica is now going to college and hopes to become a pediatrician. If you are interested in a special job, you may be able to volunteer at a company or agency which would give you more information about the job.

World Involvement

Buy Earth-Friendly Products: Encourage your family to buy products which are helpful to the environment. If you buy Ben and Jerry's Ice Cream, the Rain Forest Crunch flavor actually raises money for the rain forest. Use pump sprays instead of aerosol sprays to protect the ozone. Please use products which are biodegradable, such as paper egg cartons instead of the Styrofoam ones.

Sponsor a Child: Your family could sponsor a child from another country. My family sponsors a child from Kenya, named Jumaa, through the organization Food For The Hungry. Our money helps feed, clothe and educate Jumaa. Many families in other poor countries cannot afford to send their children to school or pay for medical care. Just a little bit of our money can make a big difference in another country. We even write to Jumaa and exchange pictures, which is very interesting. Regularly giving part of your allowance to a charity you really like can make you feel involved even when you are not personally doing something. Contact Food For The Hungry at 7729 East Greenway Rd., Scottsdale, AZ 85260; phone: 1-800-248-6437.

Get a Pen Pal: If you can, try to get a pen pal from another country. I had a pen pal in Canada and it was fun learning about her life. Having friends in other parts of the world, or even in different parts of our country, can help us understand other people's cultures.

Give a City Kid Some Fresh Air: The Fresh Air Fund is an organization that places inner city children from New York City with families on the East Coast. The children visit for two weeks in locations from Canada to Virginia. Your family may wish to host a child for two weeks in summer. Several of my friends' families have done this and they say it is fun and worthwhile. Contact Fresh Air Fund, 1040 Avenue of the Americas, New York, NY 10018; phone: 1-800-367-0003.

UNICEF: During the years I was in preschool, our school asked the students to help collect for UNICEF. While "trick-or-treating" on Halloween, I would go door to door with my parents and collect loose change from people. The money was then sent to the UNICEF association, which helps children in 140 developing countries with health care concerns, such as immunizations, clean water, nutrition and medical care. These "trick-or-treat" boxes are an easy way to help kids who need it most. Contact UNICEF, 333 E. 38th Street, 6th floor, New York, NY 10016; phone: (212) 686-5522.

Give Christmas Presents: Last year I had the best time putting together a shoe box filled with neat things for Samaritan's Purse. Samaritan's Purse is a Christian agency which collects gifts for "Operation Christmas Child," a gift-giving program which raised 1 million donated boxes for children in 36 countries. Many of the children are very poor or from countries involved in war, such as Bosnia. In many cases, these children never even get gifts, so the box is very special. I filled my girl's box with a comb, toothbrush, a small tube of toothpaste, pens, crayons, perfume, stickers and nail polish. I also wrote a letter about myself and included my picture. I then wrapped the box with pretty paper. Samaritan's Purse asked for a $5 donation to cover their shipping expenses. My brother made a box for a boy. Including the boxes that my friends put together, we shipped off 10 total!! Contact Samaritan's Purse, "Operation Christmas Child," P.O. Box 3000, Boone, NC 28607-3000; phone: (704) 262-1980.

How to Get Started

Volunteering leads to increased confidence, new friends of all ages and possible careers. I have found volunteering to be lots of fun! You can make a difference in this world. If you would like to become involved with a volunteer project, see the following list for ideas on getting started:

- churches, synagogues, schools, teachers, counselors
- civic groups like the Lions, Rotary Club, Elks
- phone book listings under volunteer opportunities
- Girl Scouts, Boys Scouts, Girls and Boys Clubs
- animal shelters and homeless shelters
- The United Way, American Red Cross and Salvation Army
- newspaper listings of volunteer positions

You can also contact:

The Boys and Girls Clubs of America

1230 West Peachtree Street, N.W.

Atlanta, GA 30309

Phone: call your local Directory Assistance for a club near you.

The American Red Cross

National Office of Volunteers: Youth Dept.

8111 Gatehouse Road, 2nd floor

Falls Church, VA 22042

Phone: (703) 206-7410

The United Way of America

701 North Fairfax Street

Alexandria, VA 22314-2045

Phone: (703) 836-7112

America's Promise—The Alliance For Youth

This is Colin Powell's volunteer organization.

They can give you information about volunteering in your area.

Phone: 1-888-555-YOUTH

Overcoming Life's Biggest Obstacles

Susan Harshfield, age 14

✂ Hobbies: *writing, reading, shopping, soccer*

📚 Favorite classes: *French and History* 📖 Favorite book: The True Confessions of Charlotte Doyle ☹ Pet peeves: *unnecessary ignorance and people who don't try anything new*

🎵 Hero: *Rosie O'Donnell* ❀ Dream: *for young people to stand up for themselves and make a difference*

I used to think, "Oh, she's so cool. I wish I could look just like that girl!" Maybe that is how you think, too. But perhaps you should really look at what you do have. You know what I mean? "That girl" might not have the most important things life has to offer. Years ago my sister was in the hospital and I wished I could get sick too, because I was jealous of all the attention she got. I've learned a lot since then. There are more important things than getting attention . . . or being skinnier . . . or having curly hair. There's health. Here's my story.

My Challenge

In first grade, my leg hurt. My mom didn't think much of it at first. She took me to the doctor. According to him, the pain at the top of my right leg was due to muscle spasms. So that is what I had for around two years, muscle spasms.

In March of 1991, I woke up to go get a drink one night. I got out of bed, but didn't get past the hallway. My stomach hurt really, really bad. I woke up my parents who took me back to the same doctor the next morning.

My doctor always thought my mom was overreacting. He didn't take the leg pains seriously enough. He sent me to the hospital because he thought I needed my appendix out. Well, he did something right.

Some of you may have guessed by now that I had cancer. Chances of living: not high. It was very far along. Somehow my pediatrician had overlooked the tumor on my pelvic bone. You've seen a grapefruit before. It was about that size — a little bigger. I'd gone about 18 months with undiagnosed Ewing's Sarcoma, which is a rare type of bone cancer.

The next few years were filled with X-rays, needles and hospital visits. Awful stuff such as getting a "port" implanted into me just below and in between my collar bones. You'll love this. It has a tube that runs under the skin and is, uh, attached to a vein just under the base of the neck. This port could be poked with an IV needle and it would only hurt when the needle went through the skin that covered the round part. Through this, they'd administer chemotherapy and take blood tests. (No more detail there, though. You might have just eaten, and I apologize.)

When I got back to Flushing after my month in Detroit, there was a pile of presents in the living room. I guess you'd call those the perks. I mean, there were so many presents, you couldn't even see the couch! My family, teachers, and friends had bombarded me with coloring books, stuffed animals, stickers, markers, posters and tons of other stuff. They bought stuff that they thought would help pass the days in the hospital that they knew were in my future. My second grade class pooled money and bought me a huge yellow duck that I immediately named Quackers. I was known at Hurley Hospital in Flint as "the little sick girl with that cute duck." I also became the owner of about 50 toy rabbits, because I'd spent Easter at the hospital.

The presents didn't make everything better. That was impossible. (They helped, though.) A few days later, I was back at the hospital under-going chemotherapy, which caused me to throw up a lot, and my hair fell out, and I was doing X-ray after boring X-ray.

It's over now. My tumor is long-since gone. I'm 14, and I have hair again. Much of those years is a jumble of mixed-up memories. For a while, when I'd look back on them, I thought I'd made it up. Then one time, in school, I was sitting there talking to another girl who'd gone through something similar. She described her hospital experience so vividly and it was so sad. I was like, "That sounds so familiar. It seems like I went through the same thing." And all of a sudden the realness of what I had gone through swept into my heart from its jail cell in my head. I could have died. They thought I would! I was like, "Whoa."

Dealing with Challenges

During my cancer treatment, my nurse, Charlotte, said that they never let anyone die without a good reason. That convinced me that since there was no reason I could remember coming up with, I was not going to die. I guess there's logic in it. My mom says that's the attitude that helps.

My sense of humor has always been my best quality. I have other reasons for still being around, though. I want to help other people, and make them happier. When something happens to you, and it's hard to deal with, you're not alone in it. And if this ever happens to you, I'm with you along with everyone else in the "club."

When my friend's grandpa died, she was quiet for a long time. She refused to talk about it. This is really common. I've been forced to talk to a few psychologists and I know that this isn't healthy. (I know, I know. Now you think that I'm a psycho. Although my friends may not agree, I think I'm pretty sane.) My friend doesn't say much about her grandpa, because he died when she was really young. She loved him, though, and if she'd *talked* about him to someone close to her, chances are that she would remember him better.

Bad things happen to everybody. I know right now as you're reading this that you can think of at least one thing that has happened that you would've liked to skip over. That's what friends are for, though. My best friends, Leslie, Dee Dee, Molly and Tonya and I all use each other to help make our problems smaller. We all depend on the other ones, and it is a good system, as long as we're not all mad at *each other*. If something happens we know there are four reliable people standing close by. It's the buddy system, and it'll get you through anything.

Something to remember, though, is when something happens to you or a friend, you can't rely on them to make things 100% better, just like they can't expect you to do that. Don't get mad at people if they can't wipe your problems away with a towel. It sounds silly, I know, but if things get really bad, sometimes it seems like people can do that, but they're holding out on you. Don't get me wrong. You can make a difference — a big one! Nobody has the power to make a life perfect, but the differences you can make for unfortunate people can help and heal, too.

Think of life as a radio station. It's your favorite station, right? (Considering the other stations.) Well, each thing that happens to you (good or bad) is a song. If you don't like the song that's on, either wait for it to end or change the station. There's probably a good song coming up, so I suggest you be patient and wait. After all, it is your favorite radio station. Oh, and the blah in between the good and bad times? Why, that's the mindless DJ babble, of course.

Sometimes it takes a sad experience to bring out who you are for real. What I mean is, a lot of girls and boys our age put up a front, and in order to uncover our personalities, it helps if you are not worried about what other people think about you. Traumatic situations cause you to look at other people without even knowing it, and you pay less attention to yourself, which isn't that bad anyway. I know. This life thing is really tough. Maybe you had a worse experience.

Bravery is important in any situation. It was important for me while I was in the hospital, but that was a different kind of bravery. It wasn't like getting the nerve to give a report in front of my class. It was courage that was forced onto me, like when you're walking alone at night. You can't turn around because you are too far away from where you used to be, and it's not in your power to make it sunny, so you just run home with your eyes half shut. People always told me that I was such "a brave little trooper." That isn't really true. They said it because I beat the odds; because I was supposed to be dead. But I didn't choose to undergo chemo. It wasn't my brave decision. I *had* to do what I did. I don't know if my parents even had the power to say no. I don't really remember being brave. I remember screaming when things didn't really hurt much, although I must have been a little brave, because here I am.

My parents think that it helps you get through something if you stay positive. I don't agree totally. I think as long as you don't assume you're a goner from the beginning of any problem, that you're gonna be fine. You don't have to be sure that everything will be fine for it to be okay in the end. You know what I mean?

Cancer and other great challenges leave physical and emotional scars that may never fade. I have scars across my stomach, some by my collar bone, and one in my heart. Well, not really in my heart, but it's there somewhere. It's in my bad moods. It's in my eyes because I see with it. It's in my dreams. This might fade away in a few years, and I am more sensitive for others, which is good, but the best and worst will always be with me.

The thing that hurts the most is growing up so fast. Sure, I know big words, but I've also been forced to see things the way an adult must see them. Everyone starts asking questions, which is tiring, and I get sympathy I no longer need. Things like this are hard to deal with. I get impatient with people easily. I often feel like I'm older than kids in my classes.

Without bad things, we wouldn't have anything to compare good things to. That would make all our emotions the same. Happy and Sad are supported by each other. If Happy takes the little step off the big cliff, Sad would be the only one left. Sad and all his little friends, like Fear, Mad, Depressed and Tantrum, are the only ones left.

Cancer is one of the many terrible things in life. At the same time, though, like all bad things, it opens windows in your mind that can make your view of everything better. "Bad" experiences make you stronger later, after the shock wears off. They just make you a person with more faces, and you become more unpredictable, a friend of Happy *and* Sad. That will leave you stationed firmly in the middle.

Tips for Overcoming What Doesn't Seem Fair

1. If you have a new problem, attack it. Just think about it as something you can only change if you want to.

2. No matter what's wrong in your life, learn as much as you can about it. If you or someone in your family got diagnosed with something, or even if there's just a big problem in your life that you don't understand, go to the library and learn as much about it as you can. Adults sometimes hide the truth, thinking that they're making things easier for you. You'll feel better knowing as much as they do, and then people will be more honest with you.

3. You're not alone. Bad things happen to almost everyone. We're all in this together. There are support systems for almost everything — from losing a pet to divorce. Get involved. You help others and they help you.

4. Don't feel sorry for yourself. I know. I know. It makes us feel better. It's not healthy. By remaining strong, you'll gain respect from yourself and everyone else.

5. It's okay to cry . . . even in front of people. I don't mean bawling at the grocery store, but sincere sadness looks much better than the forced frown that gets carved on your face when you try not to cry.

6. Bad things do happen to good people. It's not your fault. Your appendix didn't burst because you yelled at your mom.

7. Accept your obstacle and be open for suggestions. The five stages to acceptance tend to be Denial, Anger, Bargaining, Depression and Acceptance. These steps can be hard on the spirit. Become a "One Step Wonder." Try to have a cool, "so what's next?" attitude. But don't hide your feelings. Let it out when you need to yell — just not in the grocery store.

8. Don't wait for bad things and don't give up. When something difficult happens, don't throw in the towel. We'll be overcoming different things over and over forever and ever. And remember, good stuff happens just as often, if not more, and anticipating *that* is good for you.

Helping  Others

I'm here for a reason. I lived for a purpose. I am not going to stop fighting for what I believe in. I believe in getting rid of childhood disease. I am going to help people realize that they can do whatever they want. I am brave now, and I know I can do anything I want to do. Everyone can.

Open your window and let the scent of summer float in. Even if it's winter, and you feel tired and useless, all you have to do is wake up. You are in the world for a reason. Make yourself part of it. You are a girl for a reason. I'm being vague, but I am sure you know that I'm trying to tell you that when you believe in who you are, and what you do, and what you can do (anything and everything), you are at your best.

Volunteer at a nearby hospital. I'm going to as soon as I'm old enough. Probably a lot of you know, it gets sooooo boring sitting in a room by yourself. There are volunteers there, but many of them are old ladies who don't understand children. They are nice people, and it's great of them to help out, but never once did I ever see a healthy girl (besides my sister) at the hospital. It was depressing. Trust me, you could be a huge help and make some little friends. At many hospitals, when you're old enough, they even let you bring little babies to their moms. But don't forget to say hi to everyone on the pediatric floor.

My Friend Megan's Challenge

My friend Megan Lammy is 12 now, but when she was 5, she was diagnosed with "acute" Lymphocyctic Leukemia, which she says is not very "cute" (hospital humor). She was put on special chemotherapy treatment, but after two years the cancer came back. She was then put on intense treatment, but guess what? It came back again.

Her name was registered on a national list for a bone marrow transplant. Well, somewhere in the country a wonderful woman Megan doesn't know was the perfect match. She received her transplant in Seattle in

September 1995. A year later the cancer came back. They tried radiation. It came back! Megan's success is an amazement to her doctors. She's had some terrible luck, but she's still breathing! Her mother calls her a "walking miracle." That sums it up exquisitely.

I asked Megan some questions about her obstacles:

Susan: How do you feel when adults treat you differently from other kids when they learn about your situation?

Megan: I get really angry and I don't like it. I just want to be a normal kid.

Susan: Do you think it's important for people to be educated about their problems in order to understand what's happening?

Megan: Yes. My parents and doctors have always told me the truth; it's the only way I can deal with what's happening to me.

Susan: What have you learned about life from your leukemia?

Megan: Live every day to the fullest, because it could be your last. Make all your time on earth count, and be nice to everyone. I love life and I love everyone around me to the max.

Susan: What is the most important thing to remember when things aren't going your way?

Megan: Remember that it could be a lot worse, and if you just keep going it will get better. Always keep fighting, never give up!

Susan: What is your advice to girls who are left feeling hopeless and uninspired from something that has happened to them?

Megan: Nothing is ever hopeless. Look at me. I'm still alive and plan to keep fighting. Keep smiling and laughing. Life is worth living.

Do You Want to Be an Author, Too?

Here's Your Chance

Beyond Words Publishing will be compiling more *Girls Know Best* collections, and they are looking for more fantastic girl writers RIGHT NOW! If you are 6 to 16 years old and have a great chapter idea that isn't already in this book (or is different in some way), you could be one of the next girl authors. Here are the rules:

1. Your chapter idea can be from you alone, or you can work together with your sister(s) or best friend(s). (They also have to be 6 to 16 years old.)

2. Your chapter idea should be fun, unique, useful advice or activities for girls. It should also include one paragraph telling why you chose to write about that topic or how you got your idea and why it's important or (if it's an activity) fun to you.

3. Send 2-3 pages of your chapter idea (typed or clearly handwritten), a self-addressed stamped envelope (to return your chapter to you), and the *"Girls Know Best* Potential Author Questionnaire" (photocopied from the next page and filled out) to:

> Girl Writer Contest
> Beyond Words Publishing, Inc.
> 20827 N.W. Cornell Road, Suite 500
> Hillsboro, Oregon 97124-9808

4. You can also send a photo (any photo is fine) of yourself, if you want to, but a photo is optional.

BELIEVE IN YOURSELF.
GO FOR YOUR DREAMS.

Girls Know Best
Potential Author Questionnaire

PLEASE DO NOT WRITE IN THIS BOOK! Photocopy this page and fill out your information in the spaces provided. Handwritten is fine. If you can't think of an answer to something, it's okay to leave it blank. Mail your completed questionnaire with your chapter idea to Beyond Words Publishing, Inc.

Name ————————————————— **Age** ————

Address ——————————————————————

City ————————— **State** ——— **Zip Code** —————

Phone Number ( ) ————————— (to call you if you win. Beyond Words Publishing will not call you for any other reason.)

Your hobbies:

Your favorite subject or class in school:

Your favorite writer and/or book:

Your biggest pet peeve:

Your hero or role model:

Something that makes you unique:

Your dream:

Anything else you want to say:

Glossary

addiction: an uncontrollable need for and use of a substance that is known to be potentially harmful or deadly.

apathy: a lack of interest in or feelings about a particular situation; indifference.

claustrophobia: an intolerable fear of being in small, closed-in spaces.

clones: artificially-produced or developed replicas, or copies, of an original object or being.

compromise: agreement by both sides in a dispute to partially give in to the wishes of the other side.

decoupage: a craft in which decorative cut-outs, usually made of paper, are glued to a surface and covered with several coats of varnish or lacquer.

ecosystem: a community of organisms (plants, animals, bacteria, etc.) that live together in a certain natural environment.

initiative: the demonstrated ability to do things without being told what or how to do them.

intimidating: causing fear or a feeling of inferiority.

millefiori: a unique type of ornamental glass produced by cutting through bundles of multi-colored glass rods.

ornery: bad-tempered or stubborn.

perspective: the particular way a person sees or understands a situation based on his or her knowledge or background; point of view.

pervert: a person who thinks and acts in ways that are generally considered morally and socially wrong.

procrastinate: to purposely put off, usually for no good reason, doing something that needs to be done.

skirmishes: short and relatively minor fights or disagreements.

sobriety: the condition of being sober, or not under the influence of alcohol.

steep: to soak in hot, but not boiling, liquid, usually for the purpose of releasing flavor or aroma.

stereotype: an image or kind of behavior automatically assigned to a person just because he or she belongs to a certain group or class of people that might commonly show that image or behavior.

undertow: strong and dangerous water currents beneath the surface of the water that are pulling seaward when currents, or waves, at the surface appear to be moving toward the shore.

vouch: to support the truth or reliability of something said or done by someone else.

More Books to Read

Be a Super Sitter. Here's How (series). Jay Litvin and Lee Salk (NTC/Contemporary Publishing)

Best Friends: Tons of Crazy Cool Things to Do with Your Girlfriends. Melisa Albregts and Elizabeth Cape (Chicago Review)

Exploring Emotions (series). Althea Braithwaite (Gareth Stevens)

Girl Talk: Staying Strong, Feeling Good, Sticking Together. Judith Harlan (Walker)

The Girl's Guide to Life: How You Can Make the World a Great Place for Girls. Catherine Dee (Little, Brown & Co.)

Good Health Guides (series). (Gareth Stevens)

It's a Girl Thing: Dating. Mavis Jukes (Random Books for Young Readers)

The Kids' Volunteering Book. Arlene Erlbach (Lerner Publishing)

Makeup. Fashion Guide (series). Felicity Everett (EDC)

Taking Charge of My Mind and Body: A Girl's Guide to Outsmarting Alcohol, Drug, Smoking, and Eating Problems. Gladys Folkers and Jeanne Engelmann (Free Spirit)

Videos

Baby-Sitting 101, Vol. 1: The Basics and Beyond. (CarPool Productions)

Being a Friend: What Does It Mean? (Sunburst Communications, Inc.)

Girl to Woman. (United Learning, Inc.)

Lost and Found: Young People Talk about Depression. (Film Ideas, Inc.)

Web Sites

G.I.R.L. Girls Internationally wRiting Letters: a club for girls age 8-14. (worldkids.net/girl/welcom2.htm)

Girl Site. (www.girlsite.org)

Girls' Life. (www.girlslife.com)

A Girl's World Online Clubhouse. (www.agirlsworld.com)

Welcome 2 Girl Power. (www.health.org/gpower/index.htm)

To find additional Web sites, use a reliable search engine with one or more of the following keywords: *adolescence, baby-sitting, beauty, conservation, dating, depression, divorce, drugs, friends, girls, health, kids, sports, volunteering.*

Index